HELP MEET OR HINDRANCE WHICH ONE ARE YOU?

Fannie A. Pierce

Scripture verses depicting KJV, or not marked are taken from the Spirit-Filled Bible, King James Version, Copyright © 1991, 1995 by Thomas Nelson, Inc. All rights reserved.

Scripture verses depicting the NLT are taken from the Holy Bible, The New Living Translation, Copyright © 1996, 2004, Tyndale House Publishers Inc., Wheaton, IL 60189, USA. All rights reserved.

Scripture verses depicting the LB are taken from The Living Bible, Copyright © 1971, Tyndale House Publishers Inc., Wheaton, IL 60189, USA. All rights reserved.

Neil T. Anderson & Charles Mylander's quote is from their book, The Christ-Centered Marriage, Bible WordSearch Version 5/7, NavPress.

Copyright © 2010 by Fannie A. Pierce

Help Meet Or Hindrance: Which One Are You?

ISBN 978-0-9839483-2-2

Published by
Rapier Publishing Company
3417 Rainbow Parkway
Rainbow City, Alabama 35906

www.rapierpublishing.com

Printed in the United States of America

All rights reserved under the International Copyright Law. Contents and/or cover may not be reproduced in whole or in part in any form without the consent of the Publisher.

Book Cover Design: Kabraila Gray
Book Cover Picture: ISTOCK File# 115533872
Book Layout: Rapture Graphics

Acknowledgments and Thanks

To my Heavenly Father for using me for such a time as this, and for not giving up on me and loving me in spite of my unwillingness at times. Your longsuffering towards me has taught me how to be longsuffering towards others. You are my "First Love".

To my husband, Pete Pierce Jr. Thank you for twenty wonderful years and for choosing me to be your wife and to share the vision that God gave to you. After all these years, you still "rock" my world.

To my mother, Sylvia Turner, whom I greatly love, appreciate, and admire. God had the best in store for me when He chose you as my mother. Thanks for teaching me values, morals, manners, and what it means to be a women.

Special Thanks to the following women in my life who continue to make an impact.

First Lady Alethia Ramsey, (Northview Christian Church, Dothan, Alabama). When I first met you. I was broken. Your words helped me get back on focus. I greatly admire, love and appreciate you. You are truly a woman of God.

Lady Brenda Wright (United Christian Church, Gadsden, Alabama). I call you my friend. You are truly a woman of worth, power, strength and grace. Thank you for showing me how to be a lady and how to submit to my husband; not with words, but with action. You are the finest example of a woman of God who stands by her man, Apostle Maurice K. Wright.

Co-Pastor Patricia Reynolds, (Greater Vision Community Church, Killeen, Texas). You are the one who first introduced me to the word "enabler". It was you who I called when God first birth this book into my spirit. Your directness and tough love helped me more than you would ever know. You gave me the initial push I needed towards my destiny. You are also like a spiritual mother to me.

To my Editing Team:

Ty Scott-King, Taiisha Walton and Nancy Arant-Williams. Thank you for you hard work in editing this book.

Dedication

This book is dedicated to Mrs. Carolyn Howell, my mentor, my inspiration and a spiritual mother in the ministry to me.

When I needed an example of how to be a wife, it was you who the Lord used as my guide. You never gave me any words, but the Word. You never took my side, but always took His side. And when I got off track, you never judged, condemned or gave up on me, but you always said, "Dear Heart" go back to your First Love, Jesus.

Your quiet inner beauty and strength allows me to look inside of myself and yearn to be the woman of God I am called to be.

Only the Lord knows what you mean to me, because words can never express the gratitude, respect, admiration and love I have for you. You are not only a powerful and anointed woman of God, but you are a true help meet to your husband.

To me, you are the epitome of a Proverbs 31 Woman, and after all these years, you are still my example.

Love You

"Dear Heart"
Fannie

Table of Contents

Introduction xiii

Chapter One: If You Love Me... You'll Keep My Commandments 17

Chapter Two: Submission 21
    Section 1: Let's Talk About Submission 21
    Section 2: What God's Word Says About Submission
                  and Being a Help Meet 29
Section 3: Submitted (Wise) Wives in the Bible 34

Chapter Three: So You Call Yourself A Help Meet (Wife)? 39
    Section 1. Examples of a Help Meet 39
        a.   Prayer: The Greatest Asset 45
        b.   Respect Your Husband 50
        c.   Vision and Purpose 56
        d.   Stand by Your Man 61
        e.   Love Your Man 66
    Section 2. Some Characteristics of a Help Meet 70

Chapter Four: Are You A Hindrance To Your Husband? 79
    Section 1. Eve: The First Wife 79
    Section 2. Examples (Spirits) Of A Hindering Wife 85
        a.   I Want To Be the Man 88
        b.   I'm Not Your Mother, I'm Your Wife 92
        c.   He Is Not Your Daddy 96
        d.   The Know It All Wife 98
        e.   The Nagging Wife 103
        f.   The Spoiled Little Girl 107

    g.   Worldly Hindrances 110

Chapter Five: Foolish Wives In The Bible Who Hindered Their Husbands 121

Chapter Six: The Calling Of A Wife (Help Meet) 127

Conclusion 131

INTRODUCTION

When the Lord birthed this book into my spirit over six years ago, in the summer of 2007, my husband, Pete and I were going through a major transition. He had just resigned from his place of employment where he had worked faithfully for over ten years, and I was still trying to be my own woman. Little did we know that the new place the Lord was taking us to would define our destinies, individually and as a married couple.

Like Dorothy in the Wizard of Oz, what started out as a pleasant journey down the yellow brick road, soon took me to a place so unfamiliar, that I yearned to go back to what I knew, but couldn't, because I didn't know how. It was a place of isolation, regrouping and renewing. It was a place where I had to depend totally, only and earnestly on the Lord, and where I had to learn how to surrender my will to the Lord. It was a place where I had to die to self, and become what He, the Lord needed me to be—a Help Meet to my husband.

This journey was anything but easy. In fact, it was downright hard and very difficult. To give up my will, my dreams, my goals, and my desires; what I believed in, and what I was taught since I could remember and to change into someone and something else was unimaginable and unheard of. Quite frankly, I didn't want to do it even if I professed, "Lord not my will, but thine will be done." That is why the entire conversion took ten years, while completing the book took another three years. From the start to the very end it was a process of my faith to overcome my fears and doubts, as I learned to trust the Lord and allow Him to guide me through the steps on how to be a wife and help meet to my husband.

Which brings us to this book, *"Help Meet or Hindrance: Which One Are You?"* You see, I had truly perceived in my sanctified, tongue speaking, Holy-Spirit Filled, Bible toting mind that I was a bona-fide helper to my husband. And though you couldn't have convinced me otherwise, I wasn't, because in God's eyes I was in disobedience. I had to learn that a help meet is more than cooking, cleaning and yes, even intimacy.

Now, I will be the first to tell you that while writing this book, I wept and argued with God, claiming male favoritism and unfairness. To be completely honest, I didn't want to write it. To me, it appeared to give men a huge advantage (see how the world has twisted our thinking), taking women back to another era. Sometimes it was very painful to write what the Lord had put in my spirit. Yet, I knew it came directly from Him, because the more I saw it His way, the clearer I understood that I was in error of what it means to be a wife.

Believe me when I say that initially this book could go against everything you've been taught by the world, and even by religion. Yet keep in mind that God is not a religion, *"For God is Spirit, so those who worship him must worship in spirit and in truth,"* John 4:24 (NLT). Please let me clarify that this book is not a list of restrictions. It's actually designed to minister to you through the Holy Spirit.

While reading this book, you may get angry with me, thinking that I've lost my mind. I won't blame you, because I already admitted that I felt the same way too. However, I promise you, in the end, not only may it free you, but it may also help you to discover the real you—the person you were meant to be, and perhaps get you back on track with the will of God for your life.

So get some tissue and your Bible, and lets go before the Lord and allow Him to teach us how to be the help meet He created and ordained us to be.

Fannie A. Pierce

Chapter 1

If You Love Me... You'll Keep My Commandments

One Sunday while standing next to my husband in church, engulfed in praise and worship, the Lord said to me in a clear crisp voice, *"If you love me, keep my commandments."* At first, I didn't pay any attention, thinking my mind was wandering off again as it sometimes does. However, as I continued worshipping the Lord, with hands in the air and tears streaming down my face, I heard Him again, but this time more forcefully, *"If you love me, you'll keep my commandments."* It was then that I knew my mind wasn't wandering. It was the Lord speaking to me and I knew what He meant by those words. I knew what He wanted me to do. He was telling me to do something I really didn't what to do. What He'd been commanding me to do for several years—my assignment. He was asking me to be the wife and help meet my husband needed me to be. He wanted me to obey Him- die to self, and submit to my husband. And if I really loved Him, I would obey.

I shouldn't have been surprised because He'd been leading me to this place for years. A place where I must confess, I kicked, screamed and fought not to go. It was against everything I wanted. Oh sure, in my heart and in my daily confessions, I constantly cried out to Him, "Lord not my will, but thine will be done." And if truth be told, I honestly thought or perceived I was doing what He wanted me to do.

But in the year of my fortieth birthday, a change was taking place in me, a change so unfamiliar, I thought I was losing my mind. All those previous times I had said, "Lord not my will, but thine will be done," well now it was time to see if I really meant what I said.

Now don't get me wrong. Both then and now it has been my desire to do His will; however, by submitting to His will, I didn't know that it was going to cost me the very things I wanted to desperately hold on to—me, my life, my will, and my identity as a strong, independent and capable woman. While my lips and heart were saying one thing, my actions were doing the opposite of what I professed. You see, subconsciously, I didn't want to let go of my identity. I didn't want to change. Yet the closer I grew to the Lord, I understood it wasn't about me, it was all about Him and His will.

On that fateful day of my fortieth birthday, my husband threw me an elegant surprise birthday party. (I figured it out in the end, but it was still a wonderful surprise.) He had everything planned down to the last detail. Everyone was in place to make it a night I would always remember. To fool me, he told me we were going somewhere special; and, to keep the suspense at a momentum, he had recruited a couple of my dear friends to help me get ready for the big event. They came to my home, picked me up and took me to the home of one of the ladies. They were responsible for getting me ready for my big date with my husband. They pampered me so much, I felt like Queen Esther getting ready to meet her future husband, the King. There was even a beautiful new dress waiting for me. One of the ladies who assisted me was a professional hair stylist, so she did my hair and make-up. I called them my "ladies in waiting". Honestly, I am not kidding, they didn't let me do anything. They even put on my stockings for me. It was so special, but also so much fun. Once I was ready, they drove me in style to meet my husband, who at the time I thought was waiting to pick me up and take me out to dinner. It wasn't until I saw the cars parked in the rear of our destination that I knew something else was on the horizon.

When I walked into the place where my surprise party was being held, I saw all of our dear friends dressed to the nines in evening wear. But I didn't focus on them. I only had eyes for my husband. He looked so handsome and elegant in his white tuxedo. It was then that I started to cry. At first he didn't understand why I cried. Afterwards I told him that I had wept because I truly felt blessed and honored that he would go to such lengths to demonstrate not only how much he loved me, but how much he treasured me as his wife.

Towards the end of the celebration, after friends had presented their gifts and made their toasts of beautiful words (that even today I have never forgotten), it was finally my turn to speak. I thanked everyone for their kindness, love and gifts, then turning to my husband with love in my eyes and heart, I told him in front of everyone how much I thanked God for him and how much I loved and appreciated him. Now, there was nothing unusual about me speaking these words, because I had often expressed my love and appreciation to him in that manner. So, believing I was finished, I was about to sit down and enjoy the remainder of the evening, but, unknown to me the Lord had other plans. You see, I was finished, but He wasn't. The words that came out of my mouth next were not only unplanned, but I didn't want to say them at all. And I definitely did not want to say them to my husband in a room full of people. But, the Lord has a wonderful sense of humor (although at the time, I didn't see the humor).

Now in my heart, I knew the Lord was telling me to do this. He'd been telling me for some time, yet I'd never said it out loud to anyone, especially not my husband. Frankly, because I didn't want to obey the Lord in this area, I kept these things to myself, hoping the prompting would pass. You see, I never told my husband that my assignment was to be his wife, his help meet, and to assist him to be the man God called him to be. I never told him that I was called to give up my career, dreams, and desires, and to focus on his dreams, his goals, and his vision. I'd never told him how the Lord had pressed into my spirit to pray for him, to keep my mouth shut, and just be his wife. Call it pride, or fear that I might appear like a weak, helpless female to him, my family and friends, but I'd never told him. However, that night on my fortieth birthday, through the power of the Holy Spirit, in front of all of our friends—that night I told him what the Lord had assigned me to do. (I didn't even know what I said until weeks later when someone from the party told me how much I blessed them with my words).

I wish I could say from that moment on we lived happily ever after, like they do in fairy tales, but I can't. We didn't. In spite of the words I had spoken, my flesh didn't want to let go. It didn't want to die. It wanted to fight to the end. It wanted to take back those words that I thought were so unfair. Why had the Lord called me to do this? Why did He choose my day of celebration to have me say something that He knew I didn't want to say? What I didn't comprehend at that time, was on that night of my fortieth birthday a spiritual change was taking place within me. It was the beginning of my assignment, my calling. To die to self, obey God, submit to my husband, and be the helpmeet He intended for me to be.

For the next three years, the Lord only told me to do three things. That's right, only three: (1) Get into Him (His Word). (2) Write (to keep me sane and occupied), and (3) Pray for my husband and be his wife. Did I stay on my assignment? I must sadly confess that for the most part, I didn't. Like I told you, my flesh didn't want to die, and as you read the book, you'll see why. For those three years, I did everything but help my husband. He didn't know this. No one knew. To people, I was the perfect wife; however, I wasn't. I was in rebellion. I had refused my assignment. And the Lord knew this. And that was why, on that particular Sunday, He addressed me with those words, "If you love me, you'll keep my commandments."

Chapter 2

Submission

Section 1. Let's Talk About Submission

For the most part in our society today, if a woman hears the words (especially from a man), "You must submit to your husband," she tends to look at you like you have lost your complete mind. If you are not careful, she may tell you where you can find it, and not always in the most pleasant lady-like manner. To many women, *submission* is a dirty word. Don't laugh. I am not talking about the world. I'm talking about Christian women. For you see, the religious sector has made the very idea of submitting to one's husband a disagreeable and undesirable task. It puts us in the mindset of bondage, or worse, the Stone Age, when cavemen would beat their wives over the head with a club, while dragging them into the cave.

From the very beginning, we hear the words preached loud and clear from the pulpit, "Wives you must submit to your husband. You must do what he tells you to do." Well, in a sense this is true, but not in the manner that we are taught. Unfortunately, rarely is the rest of the scripture preached which says, *"... Husbands, love your wives, even as Christ also loved the church, and gave himself for it,"* Ephesians 5:25. I promise you I am not male bashing, or bashing the church. What I am saying is that as the Body of Christ, we have not been instructed on the true meaning of relationship and submission as it pertains to husbands and wives.

As I said earlier, I had a real problem with submission. Not necessarily scripturally, but the way that it was taught to me. It wasn't until God gave me the revelation or insight (which by the way, I gained the hard way, because I had a hard head), that I was able to come into the full knowledge and understanding on how to submit to my husband. But before I continue, let me tell you of another incident that happened on the same day the Lord told me to obey His commandments.

Do you remember in the previous chapter, when I told you how during praise and worship, the Lord spoke to me about submitting to my husband, *"If you love me you'll keep my commandments,"* John 14:15. Well, later that day, my husband and I went out to dinner with another couple from church. Driving home from the restaurant, we began to engage in a friendly conversation. However, in the midst of the conversation, things began to get a little heated. As a result my husband Pete's tone and words were suddenly harsh and angry. In fact, he was downright belligerent. Though he wasn't aware of his tone, the others heard it too. The only thought going through my mind was: *"How dare him! After a powerful encounter with the Lord earlier, now he is being mean to me. I'm trying to die to self and be nice, and he has the nerve to speak harshly to me in front of others."*

As you can imagine, I was furious. But the gentle whisper of the Holy Spirit said, "Let it go." It took every bit of self-control in me not to go off on him in anger; because in my sanctified mind and to save face in front of the others, I believed I had the right. Yet, I didn't say anything. I rode home the rest of the way in silence. When we arrived at the house, I feigned tiredness and went to our bedroom. Once there, like a hurt, rejected child, I immediately started raving, ranting and crying out to the Lord about Pete's behavior.

In tears, I told the Lord, "Now listen Lord, I didn't do anything to Pete. In fact, I was being nice to him, too nice for him to disrespect and humiliate me in front of our friends. And you want me to submit to him? You want me to be nice to him and pray for him after what he did to me?" I went on for at least ten minutes. After I had my little temper tantrum, the Lord finally comforted me with His gentle and soothing words, *"I know, but I promise you it's going to be alright."* How could I argue with God? Feeling that I had no other choice, still hurt and in tears, I went to sleep. You would have thought that after that incident it would've become easier to submit, but that was just the beginning. It actually got worse. I told you I was dying to flesh. Oh by the way, the Lord convicted Pete for speaking harshly to me. After I woke up from my nap, he came into the room and apologized.

Now, with that story in mind, let's talk about submission. First and foremost, we should know that it is God and not man who commands women to submit to their husbands. Regardless of how we think, or feel about the idea, as Christian married women we don't have an option. It's right there in the Word of God. I know some of you may be saying, "But the Bible was written by men; therefore, it is based on a man's perspective rather than that of a woman." Or you might also be saying, "Fannie, I want to submit, but you don't know my husband." True, I don't know your husband, but I do know what the word of God says, and we can make one of two choices- either obey or disobey. And as for the Bible being written by men, yes it was; however, it was written by and with the inspiration, revelation, and guidance of the Holy Spirit, *"For the prophecy came not in old time by the will of man: but holy men of God spake as they were moved by the Holy Ghost,"* 2 Peter 1:21. The point is we cannot argue with God or His Word if we desire to walk in His will.

I believe the core of the problem lies beyond submitting to our husbands, and that is—we need to be properly taught the biblical principles on submission. If we are correctly taught the biblical principles on why God commands us to submit, we wouldn't have a problem. After all, we all want to please Jesus. If we had been properly taught, we would understand that in submitting to our husbands, we are actually submitting unto the Lord. When we finally grasp the truth on this, we will see it as an honor and privilege to submit. Then not only will Jesus be pleased with us, but He will bless us for our obedience.

Allow me to give you an example. One day a female employee came to speak to me about a work-related incident. I was the Human Resources Director at a healthcare facility, so it was not unusual for me to counsel employees on job-related issues. As I began counseling her, it was soon discovered that her personal life was interfering with her job performance. Because I am a Christian, I asked her what was wrong. During the course of the conversation the subject of submission came up. By her conversation, I knew she was having problems with submitting to her husband, mainly because she didn't quite understand its concept. She started telling me that she knew she had to submit to her husband (cooking, cleaning, etc.), but she was clearly struggling. Unfortunately, she was basing her knowledge on submission on how another woman of authority submitted to her husband. That was her first mistake.

I know as women, we tend to look at how prominent mature women of faith relate to their husbands, and model our behavior after them. This is not entirely a bad thing to do; however, what we fail to understand is that we are not married to those women's husbands. We are married to our own husband, and each one is different. I know my husband is anyway. I can't base the way I submit to Pete on how another woman submits to her husband. I have to submit to Pete based on Pete's needs, personality and make-up. We must have a good understanding on this concept before we can accept the necessity to submit.

Do you have to submit the way another woman submits to her husband? The truth is you cannot. You are not married to that individual. Hopefully, your marriage foundation is derived from God and His Word; therefore, He will tell you how you need to submit to your husband. Of course it will be according to scriptural principals and divine order. Shame on anyone who says you have to do it my way because it's the only true and right way. Not only are those individuals wrong, but they are putting God's people in bondage. People can provide you godly spiritual guidance on submitting. In fact, I encourage women (especially those who have recently gotten married) to go to the mature spiritual women in their church or in their lives for godly wisdom and guidance on how to be a wife and how to submit to one's husband. However, we are to provide only wisdom and guidance, based on God's Word. The "girlfriend" mentality that says, "I would do this or that" kind of wisdom or guidance is wrong, especially if you are seeking advice from a woman who is not married. As my grandmother would say, "How can an unmarried woman tell a married woman about her husband? She doesn't have a man!"

Back to the young lady who had a submission problem, I gently told her in a motherly fashion, "Honey, find out what pleases your husband. His likes and dislikes. If you don't know, ask him, or ask God. Then pray and ask God for help, and then submit to those things that the Lord and your husband need you to." Don't get in bondage because someone else told you to do it a certain way.

It clearly states in the Word, *Wives, submit yourselves unto your own husbands, as unto the Lord,"* Ephesians 5:22. Note that it doesn't state submit to another man. It says submit to your own husband. Just because another woman's husband requires her to cook everyday, doesn't mean you must do as she does- unless your husband requires it. Your only responsibility is to please your husband. Pete doesn't need or even want me to cook everyday. However, I know that when he goes somewhere, he wants me to go with him. He doesn't know that sometimes I prefer to stay at home because I have learned to submit in this area. I'm not married to anyone else, but Pete. Therefore, I answer to Pete and the Lord. Another thing that we will discuss further in upcoming chapters is that you never submit to another man if you cannot submit to your husband. In doing so, you are not honoring your husband, and the Lord is not pleased. I don't care who he is, your boss, or a King. Other than the Lord, your husband is first. This is the order of God.

During some intense days while I was learning to die to my flesh, my husband and I counseled a particular couple with similar issues as ours. After listening to them it was very clear that they still loved each other very much, but what they had was a failure to communi cate—meaning that over time, their communication lines shut down to a point where they stopped listening to each other. When they did communicate, all they did was argue. After listening to both of their concerns objectively, Pete and I began to counsel the couple. He spoke first (I had to learn how to let him do this too). When it was my turn to speak, with the guidance of the Holy Spirit, I explained to the wife the order of God pertaining to the husband and wife. I then encouraged her to cover her husband in prayer, then to submit and let the Lord take control. With tears in her eyes, she replied, "You don't understand. I do those things, and he is still the same way."

As painful as it was for me, I had to tell her something I knew she didn't want to hear; but, I knew that if I didn't, I would be doing her an injustice by pacifying the situation. So I gently, but firmly said, "I know. I felt the same pain. And I also thought it was unfair. But you must die to your flesh and submit to your husband. When you do your part, you can trust God to take care of your husband." We never want to hear these things, but what more can we tell people other than the truth of God's Word.

Often times as women (I include myself), we think God is unfair, especially when we want our own way, or we're feeling sorry for ourselves. Now I am not saying that you have to submit to your husband if he is out of order, such as abusive in any kind of way or engaging in extra marital affairs. The same is true if he is telling you to do something illegal. We have to use godly wisdom on matters like these. However, if your husband is a man of God, living holy and righteous, it is your wifely duty (yes I said it- duty) before the Lord to submit to him. As I said earlier, whether we want to believe it or not, as Christians we have no other option or choice but to walk in God's perfect will and order. If we choose not to submit, we are in abject rebellion.

I would be telling you an untruth if I said that this issue wasn't difficult for me. Submitting to my husband was one of the most challenging aspects of my Christian walk. That's because in essence, it means dying to self so another can live. I can recall, literally crying before the Lord when I finally got it after ten long years; weeping as I felt my flesh actually dying in the physical sense. The pain was so excruciating that I wanted to scream. Yes, it hurt that bad! And the enemy knew it, because it was during this process that my husband changed from Dr. Jekyll to Mr. Hyde. From my point of view, my sweet, lovable husband became a mean, self-absorbed man I barely knew. His tone became overtly hostile, and he was everything but nice to me. Although he will deny this accusation, it was true, or at least that's the way I perceived him. Interestingly enough, the meaner he became, the more the Lord told me to be quiet. During this process, I felt more like his slave than his wife.

But after ten years, I finally got it. Or maybe I should say that I got tired of fighting my destiny. I yielded to Jesus, the Author and Finisher of my faith, and began focusing on what He had done for me. He had to submit to death on the cross so that I could live. His cost was much greater than mine could ever be. There are no words in the human language to accurately describe His agony. It was not something He looked forward to doing; it was hard. So hard, He prayed to the Father three times, *"Father, if you are willing, please take away this cup of horror from me. But I want your will, not mine,"* Luke 22:42 (Living Bible). The process of dying was so intense that His sweat became blood. And yet in spite of this, He did it. Jesus loved me enough to die for me so I can live. He wasn't concerned about His life. He was only concerned about my life. This is what I finally came to realize. In order for my husband to live his fullest in Christ and to reach his destiny, I had to die to self.

If anyone tells you it was easy to die to self, or it was easy to give up his/her will, I want to meet that person, because it certainly was not easy for me. Any sacrifice, especially the dying of your will is extremely painful. If it doesn't cause you pain, it may not be a sacrifice at all.

The days when Pete turned into Dr. Hyde, I couldn't say anything, even when both the Lord and I knew he was wrong. I had to obey God and keep my mouth shut. During those times, I felt like the biggest fool who ever lived. Inside, I was in deep emotional pain, and desperately wanted to burst into tears, which I did often during this process. I couldn't let him know that I was hurting, or make him aware of what I was going through. All I could think of was that I had to die to self, so Pete could live.

And this is what a help meet is—someone who helps another reach his/her destiny. If you think about it, at some time or another, whether single, married, or widowed, we have all been help meets to someone. You are a help meet to your students if you are a teacher, to your boss if you work at a job or to your patients if you're a healthcare provider.

What greater role or gift can a wife give her husband than to help him be all God called him to be? What a joy and a privilege it is to know that the Lord assigned women to assist their husbands in running His Kingdom.

Now let's see what the Word has to say on the subject.

Section 2. What God's Word Says About Submission and Being a Help Meet

If you are a born again believer, the Bible (the Word of God) should be your training manual and source of wisdom regarding how to live. No matter what the world says, the Bible is not antiquated; it is still just as practical and predictable as it was over 2000 years ago. We can make excuses and justify it to make it fit into our plans; but, regardless of how we might argue the point, if we say that we believe the Word and are Christians, we have no choice but to obey it. There is no gray area.

While that may be hard to take, it is the truth. And we as the Body of Christ must get back to the truth, which is the Word of God. Bottom-line, God wants us to lay down our lives. In Matthew 16:24 (NLT) it states, *"Then Jesus said to the disciples, "If any of you wants to be my follower, you must put aside your selfish ambition, shoulder your cross, and follow me."* Once we understand that our bodies are not our own, and that they belong to God, we will not have a problem dying to ourselves, and submitting one to another.

We are help meets when we obey God's Word and hindrances when we disobey. Ladies, please again I ask you not to shoot me down. These are not my words. They are from God's Word. I too wish it was another way, yet there is not; therefore, I cannot, nor will I, make an apology for what thus said the Lord. Before we continue, let me repeat, we as women cannot focus on if our husbands are in compliance. Rather, we need to focus on our role and responsibility in the matter. If we take care of God's business, He will take care of ours.

Here is what the Word of God says about submission:

"And the Lord God said, It is not good that the man should be alone; I will make him an help meet for him," Genesis 2:18.

"And the Lord God caused a deep sleep to fall upon Adam and he slept: and he took one of his ribs, and closed up the flesh instead thereof; [22] And the rib, which the Lord God had taken from man, made he a woman, and brought her unto the man. [23] And Adam said, This is now bone of my bones, and flesh of my flesh: she shall be called Woman, because she was taken out of Man. [24] Therefore shall a man leave his father and his mother, and shall cleave unto his wife: and they shall be one flesh," Genesis 2:21-24.

"Like Adam, the woman was not spoken into existence as was all the rest of creation. Unlike Adam, however, she was not an independent creature taken from the dust. She was related to man in creation. God formed the woman from a part of the man. Adam knew the difference instantly and proclaimed, *"This is now bone of my bones and flesh of my flesh; she shall be called 'woman,' for she was taken out of man,"* Genesis 2:23. The woman was not created to have an independent status from man, and no longer does man have an independent status from her. They were not created to be in competition with each other. Eve came into being by the power of God, from man, for whom she is called to be a helpmate. She is the only suitable helper for him."[1]

Let's look at it this way. God understands that the task He gave to man was not to be completed by a lone individual. Therefore, He provided man with the assistance he needed to get the job done. He knew man needed someone, so He created woman. Woman was designed to compliment man, to help him, not to compete with, or be independent from him. What man lacked, she provided, and what she lacked, man provided. They both needed each other to fulfill their destiny, and to complete their assignment.

"So God created man in his own image, in the image of God created he him; male and female created he them. [28] And God blessed them, and God said unto them, Be fruitful, and multiply, and replenish the earth, and subdue it: and have dominion over the fish of the sea, and over the fowl of the air, and over every living thing that moveth upon the earth," Genesis 1:27-28.

1

Man wasn't created for woman; woman was created for man. In God's eyes, this was and still is a good thing. The only reason we cannot perceive this is because the world has distorted our thinking and vision on the topic. The woman was to be a "helper" (Hebrew: *ezer kenegdo*) to her husband. She wasn't a replica, nor was she inferior to him. She was created to complement him. She was the perfect solution to man, and the plan of God. God's intent for them and for the marriage was to be fruitful and replenish the earth. They both were needed to accomplish this because separately they couldn't do it alone, but as a team they could—thus two becoming one. God's plan for the marriage was bigger than both of them; therefore, He needed both of them. His plan for the marriage has not changed. He still needs both the man and the woman working together to accomplish something bigger than each of them could do alone.

Husbands need a help meet to accomplish their God-given assignment. Or let me put it this way, husbands need a submissive help meet to accomplish their God-given assignment. This brings us to the subject of submission. Here is what the Word of God says pertaining to wives submitting unto their husbands:

"Wives, submit yourselves unto your own husbands, as unto the Lord. [23] For the husband is the head of the wife, even as Christ is the head of the church: and he is the saviour of the body. [24] Therefore as the church is subject unto Christ, so let the wives be to their own husbands in everything," Ephesians 5:22-24.

"Wives, submit yourselves unto your own husbands, as it is fit in the Lord," Colossians 3:18.

Submission is beautiful when you view it the way God created it to be. One author puts it so eloquently, "The spirit of submission, whereby a woman voluntarily acknowledges her husband's leadership responsibility under God is an act of faith. The Bible nowhere "submits" or subordinates women to men, generically. Therefore the woman submits herself unto her husband, and the husband is charged to lovingly give himself to caring for his wife—never exploiting the trust of her submission. This divine order was never shown, or given to reduce the potential, purpose, or fulfillment of women." [2]

With all this revelation, the question is, "Why do we have a hard time submitting to our husbands?" The answer is deeper than you think. For many of us, we don't submit because we have a trust issue. We are afraid to completely trust God with our lives. We are afraid of totally surrendering our lives and will. And it's understandable because giving up one's total life, and allowing someone else to guide and lead you to an unknown territory is a hard thing to do. Even the most matured Christians can find this difficult to obtain. However, if we can't totally put our trust in God, then how can we totally trust our husbands? Wives who are fearful of true submission are not putting their total trust in God. The Word clearly says in Proverbs 3:5 to, *"Trust in the Lord with all thy heart and lean not on thy own understanding."*

Two key factors here include: (1) Trusting in the Lord and (2) Leaning not on our own understanding. In order to trust the Lord completely, we mustn't try to understand, or attempt to figure it out. Rather, we must just obey. This is where I had problems, and where I believe others also have problems. The Spirit in us wants us to obey and trust in God, but the flesh and our mind want us to do the opposite. If left to our own devices, we as humans always want it our way.

I wanted to trust the Lord, yet I was afraid. I felt that if I gave in and obeyed, I would lose myself and my identity. I was afraid to surrender my all- my desires, my dreams, my goals, and my traditions to another person. The only way I knew was the way that I had always been, and the way that I had always done things. In my mind, I kept thinking, "If I surrendered my all, who would I be upon my surrender? What would become of me? Who would I become? Suppose that person would not appreciate what I did? Suppose he would treat me differently?" Suppose, suppose, suppose. All of these suppositions kept me from fulfilling my assignment, resulting in wasted years of agony, turmoil, pain and defeat. It came down to this main factor; I didn't trust God with my life. I didn't believe that He would take care of me—that He had my back.

No I am not ashamed to admit that I was afraid. However, I knew what the Word said; therefore, as much as I wanted another way out, I didn't have an option because the Word of God says: And the LORD God said, *"Wives, submit yourselves unto your own husbands, as unto the Lord. [23] For the husband is the head of the wife, even as Christ is the head of the church: and he is the saviour of the body. [24] Therefore as the church is subject unto Christ, so let the wives be to their own husbands in everything,"* Ephesians 5:22-24.

Section 3. Submitted (Wise) Wives in the Bible

The Bible says that a wise woman builds her house (Proverbs 14:1). In other words, a woman who is submitted to her husband according to God's Word builds her house and the Lord is pleased with her.

A woman who trusts the Lord completely can easily submit to her husband. Not because of her husband, but because she knows Her Father and He always takes very good care of her. You don't believe me? OK, well, the following is a list of five women from the Bible who understood the true calling of submission. Their lives are forever depicted in the Bible as great heroines of faith, strength, beauty, grace and dignity. Were they perfect? No. They just trusted God.

1. Sarah *(See Genesis 12 – Genesis 23:1)*

God told Abram (later called Abraham) to leave his country, family and friends and follow Him. When Abram told Sara, his wife (later called Sarah), she didn't hesitate. She followed her husband. Through all the frustrations, setbacks, and mistakes (twice out of fear for his life Abraham gave her to other men), she still stood with him. As a result, she carried the seed of the great nation of Israel, God's chosen people. She is as a specific example of a woman who was submissive to her husband, so much so that out of respect she called him her master. That is, she recognized and reverenced him as the leader and head of their household (Genesis18:12 and 1 Peter 3:6). Sarah didn't put her trust in her husband per se; she put her trust in God. The rest is history.

2. Esther *(See the Book of Esther)*:

Here is the verse that changed the destiny of Esther and her people:

"Don't think for a moment that you will escape there in the palace when all other Jews are killed. [14] If you keep quiet at a time like this,

deliverance for the Jews will arise from some other place, but you and your relatives will die. What's more, who can say but that you have been elevated to the palace for just such a time as this?" Esther 4:13-14 (NLT).

Esther's submission to her uncle allowed her to have favor with her husband, the King. As a result, her people's lives were spared. She brought honor to God, her people and her husband. However, before Esther could have requested an appointment with the king, she learned to submit to the man—her husband, who just so happened to be the king. By doing this she was given divine favor even when she went against protocol. She could have never received this type of favor if she wasn't a submitted wife.

3. Ruth *(See the Book of Ruth)*:

Because of her submission to her mother-in-law Naomi (her deceased husband's mother) and Naomi's God, Ruth not only came to the attention of her future husband Boaz (a wealthy man), but she became part of the lineage of Jesus Christ. Ruth was the great-grandmother of King David. (You may not see the results of your submission in your lifetime, but always know when you obey God, your legacy lives on to tell your success story).

4. Abigail *(See 1 Samuel 25:1-42)*:

And there was a man in Maon, whose possessions were in Carmel; and the man was very great, and he had three thousand sheep, and a thousand goats: and he was shearing his sheep in Carmel. [3] Now the name of the man was Nabal; and the name of his wife Abigail: and she was a woman of good understanding, and of a beautiful countenance: but the man was churlish and evil in his doings; and he was of the house of Caleb. And David heard in the wilderness that Nabal did shear his sheep. [5] And David sent out ten young men, and David said unto the young men, Get you up to Carmel, and go to Nabal, and greet him in my name: [6] And thus shall ye say to him that liveth in prosperity, Peace be both to thee, and peace be to thine house, and peace be unto all that thou hast. [7] And now I have heard that thou hast shearers: now thy shepherds which were with us, we hurt them not, neither was there ought missing unto them, all the while they were in Carmel. [8] Ask thy young men, and they will shew thee. Wherefore let the young men find favour in thine eyes: for we come in a good day: give, I pray thee, whatsoever cometh to thine hand unto thy servants, and to thy son David. [9] And when David's young men came, they spake to Nabal according to all those words in the name of David, and ceased. [10] And Nabal answered David's servants, and said, Who is David? and who is the son of Jesse? there be many servants now a days that break away every man from his master. [11] Shall I then take my bread, and my water, and my flesh that I have killed for my shearers, and give it unto men, whom I know not whence they be?," 1 Samuel 25:2-11.

Abigail had a cruel and dishonest husband, yet she still submitted to him in spite of his character. When David inquired of provisions of Nabal, Abigail's husband harshly refused. In anger, David wanted to slay him and his entire household: *"Get your swords!" was David's reply as he strapped on his own. Four hundred men started off with David, and two hundred remained behind to guard their equipment,"* 1 Samuel 25:13 (NLT). (David was angry because he protected Nabel's flock and shepherds while they were shearing. In those days it was custom that the flock owner would reward such kindness with provisions of food and drink. Nabal's rude refusal provoked David to anger.)

Abigail, being a wise woman, went to David with the provision he had requested. Still honoring her husband, despite knowing the repercussions, she informed him later of what she had done. In Nabel's anger of what she did, he fell ill, and died days later. David hearing of this went to her and she became his wife. In the end, she kept David from sinning by killing a man out of anger. Abigail was wise because even when her husband was difficult to live with and evil in his doing, she submitted to him. In spite of her husband's surly disposition, the Bible says that Abigail was a woman of good understanding and beautiful countenance. Her submission brought bountiful blessings in the end. (Be mindful, Abigail's husband was surly and difficult, and not abusive- there is a difference.)

5. Mary, Mother of Jesus *(See Matthew, Mark, Luke & John, The Four Gospels)*:

Mary responded, *"I am the Lord's servant, and I am willing to accept whatever he wants. May everything you have said come true." And then the angel left,"* Luke 1:38 (NLT).

Mary, the perfect example of a wise and submitted woman, submitted without hesitation when confronted by the Angel of the Lord. She didn't need to know how or why; she trusted God. As a result, hers was the highest honor ever given to a woman. She is the mother of our Lord and Savior Jesus Christ.

Mary understood the consequences of her decision. In that era, if an unmarried woman was found to be with child she was stoned, or put away. By law, Joseph, had the authority to stone her or put her away. Yet, even knowing the outcome, she submitted to that authority. Laying aside her concern, she chose to trust that God would take care of the situation. And the Lord did exactly that.

All of these women had different circumstances, problems, and issues, and yet they all trusted God to take care of them and their situation and He did. They gave up everything, but in the end, they gained so much more in return. If they were alive today, I wonder what these great women of faith would have to say to us about today's woman's view on submission.

I know what many of us would say to these women. Taking on the "girlfriend" or "sister" mentality, we would probably call them crazy for taking that kind of abuse, particularly in Sarah's case. We would probably tell them how today's women don't believe in taking any *"nonsense"* from a man, including our husbands, and how we definitely don't believe in submitting to them. We would tell them how we don't have to submit because we can buy our own things, with our own money, from our own jobs. We may even go as far as saying we don't need a man because we can take care of ourselves. Yes, we may have a lot to say.

Back in the 70's, there was a commercial about women that stated *"We've come a long way baby."* Yes, perhaps we have. Yet, I can't help but wonder if we've digressed instead of progressed.

Chapter 3

So You Call Yourself A Help Meet (Wife)?

Section 1. Examples of a Help Meet

Now that we have a better understanding of what the Word says about being a help meet or wife, let's talk about some other factors involved in being a help meet. Let's look at some everyday things that you may or may not be aware of, but are essential to your role as a wife and to the growth of both your marriage and your spirituality. Before I go on, to keep you from getting into bondage, let me explain once again that a help meet is not a doormat, slave, or second-class citizen to her husband. This is not only against God's Word and order, but it is very unhealthy. If this is the status of your marriage or your analogy of what a help meet is, then *Hallelujah* my sister, help is on the way. If you surrender to God, accept His ways and pray for your husband, He will change your circumstances. However, don't give Him a time limit like I did. Instead, just be patient and gentle while you wait for His answer. The Lord will come through in His timing.

As I mentioned earlier, my interpretation of a help meet was cooking, cleaning, washing clothes, helping with the bills and taking care of his intimate needs. I had those parts down. I guess that's why it was so hard for me to fully comprehend what the Lord meant when He kept telling me to submit to Pete. I would respond by saying, "I am. What more do you want me to do?" I was frustrated with the Lord and angry at Pete, not realizing that the problem was with me and my state of rebellion. In my sanctified mind, I kept telling the Lord (through my actions) I didn't feel I needed to change. In my opinion, my husband was the one with the problem. I argued, "It's Pete. It's him, not me. So why are you telling me to change?" I'm not kidding! For five years I would say, "Lord, look at Pete. He's wrong, and you don't get on him about it, but oh, you're always getting on me. It's not fair." Sounds childish, doesn't it? Yet this is where I was. And in my really bad days (which I am ashamed to admit were many) I said, "Lord, don't you hear me or even care about me anymore. It's Pete, it's not me. Get on him for a change." I'm serious when I say it seemed like the Lord was always getting on me and not my husband. (I told you I was really struggling.)

Even when Pete wouldn't pick up after himself, the Lord got on me. All he had to do was pick up after himself, yet he made absolutely no effort to do so. Over and over I would tell him, but he still wouldn't pick up after himself. Now before I go on, I want to point out that this is one of my biggest pet peeves, which I constantly reminded him about it, so he knew. However, when I would mention it to him, he would look at me innocently and say, "I forgot." Now understand, I really love my husband, but on those occasions, I wanted to hit him, and hit him very hard. But you know what the Lord would tell me? He would tell me to pick up the stuff and be quiet. Once again I would ask, "Lord why are you always picking on me and not getting after Pete?" His response would be, *"You are worrying about a penny-anny (a term we used in Baltimore growing up on the block) piece of paper that's not worth arguing about."* Ouch! The Lord sure does know how to make you see how immature and small you really are. This battle, however insignificant it may seem, went on for years.

I could not accept the fact that the Lord wanted me to continue to give up everything, but didn't expect Pete to do likewise. After all, I gave up my career. Wasn't that enough? I had been doing great things as a successful captain in the Unites States Army. I truly loved being a soldier, being all I could be. When I met Pete, I had just come out of a terrible divorce, and to be frank, at the time I didn't want to remarry. But the minute I saw Pete, I am not kidding, I knew that he would be my husband. I fell in love with him the same week I met him. Pete felt the same way about me too. So, after be ing single for eighteen months, we went through marriage counseling with my deacons, my Elder and a host of Christian friends, we got married on October 16, 1993. (We'd met in June. He'd proposed three weeks later and four months later, we were married.)

The first three years were blissfully happy. I was doing my thing; he was doing his. During that time the Lord said nothing about change. Both Pete and I were successful military professionals. He was a senior non-commissioned officer and I was an officer. I outranked him, but that didn't matter. I loved the fact that I was making money and contributing to the family.

In the third year of our marriage, strange things began to happen. The Lord kept pressing in my spirit to get out of the army. Totally shocked and dumbfounded by what I was hearing, my reply was, "What? You want me to do want?" Now, if anyone loved the military, it was me. I was the personification of an officer. In ROTC at Bowie State College (now University) I was the Battalion Commander, which was the highest rank a cadet could obtain. I won numerous awards, and had many prestigious assignments. I was good at being a soldier and had planned to make a career out of the army. So, when the quiet voice of the Holy Spirit began to move me in this direction, I cried and fought against it.

A year later, I finally obeyed. However, I found a way around getting out entirely, and that was by joining the Army National Guard. I was still in the army, just not the regular army. I was still Captain Pierce. And not only was I in the National Guard, but I'd also acquired a position at the army base teaching soldiers. I was getting paid double for what I secretly loved and craved—power and success, and of course the army. I could still say, "Look at me. I am the quintessence of a successful woman." Although I didn't say this out loud, subconsciously that is what I was thinking.

In that same year, came change two. Pete got orders to Fort McClel lan, Alabama. We moved, and my life has never been the same. Now I can see that it was for our good; however, in the beginning, the process was like hell on earth to me. Everything that I had worked for, everything that I wanted to be, ceased to exist the moment we crossed the Alabama state line. Strangely, when I drove into Alabama (we were in separate cars), my tape player skipped (which it has never done before or since) to a particular worship song that I loved. I should have known something was about to happen, because it was at that moment, a strange feeling came over me, and out of nowhere, I started to bawl like a newborn baby.

The first five years in Alabama were hard for me, but for Pete, life had never been so good. During that first year, I hunted everywhere for work but found nothing. Now looking back, I know it was the Lord's doing. He closed all the doors I tried to walk through. You would have thought I would've gotten the picture, but oh no, not me. I still wanted my way. After about nine months of begging and pleading to the Lord to let me have a job, I finally got one making $8.50 an hour. I am not joking! I went from $45,000.00(+) a year to $8.50 an hour. Here I was, Captain Pierce, a military officer, the crème of the crème with a college degree, making $8.50 an hour. Talk about an insult. The Lord was humbling me at the time, I just wasn't aware of it.

Also, one thing I was always proud of was my excellent credit rating. During those nine months, my A+ credit went from a C to a D, and finally to an F. Eventually I had to file bankruptcy. While we didn't lose homes, or cars, I lost my excellent credit rating. This was one more area in which the Lord was breaking me. So when I got the job for $8.50, I thought I was rich.

The Lord broke my stubborn will in many other areas too. For instance, in the past when people would tell me that they didn't have $5.00, I would look at them weird and say, "It's only $5.00." Yet, when I didn't have $5.00 it wasn't so weird. I understood. It continued to get worse. In the past, I always had the money to pay our bills, especially the utilities. But things were so bad financially, I had to go to the local power company and fill out the paperwork for budget billing. I was never so humiliated, and it didn't help that the customer service woman was very rude to me. I left in tears, pleading to the Lord to stop punishing me.

On one occasion we didn't have the money to pay our water bill. Mindful, it was only $40.00. We had to go out of town, so we'd asked a married couple who'd became our good friends to watch the house and feed our dog. Upon returning, we noticed an envelope on the end table in the living room that contained forty dollars and a note which said, "We were led to bless you and pay this bill." (In our rush to get on the road, I had unknowingly left the bill on the table.) Pete just held me as I burst into tears and thanked God for His blessings. It was only $40.00, but at that time it felt like a thousand dollars. For the first time, my pride wasn't in the way. I wasn't ashamed to take the money. Our friends may never realize the breakthrough we received that day because of their generous gift.

All of the incidents I just mentioned were major to me, but the most life changing and traumatic event, during that time was the shifting of order in our home. For the first time in my entire adult life, I had to depend on a man- something I promised myself I would never do, regardless if I was married or not. Growing up in a single-parent household on social services, I made a vow when I was young, like Scarlet O'Hara did in "Gone With The Wind," only mine was, "I will never depend on a man. I am my own woman."

Some people say that the Lord has a sense of humor. I believe that too (although back then I didn't think it was humorous). Our all-wise and knowing Father must've smiled on me when I made that statement about never depending on a man. He already knew that one day not only would those words come back to haunt me, but I would have to eat them. For the first time, I had to depend on my husband for income. No longer could I go shopping at my favorite department stores or any other stores without consulting him first.

And he usually refused my request. Not because he was being mean, we just didn't have the money. For nine months I became a stay at home wife. And you know what? It wasn't bad. I actually enjoyed being at home. Although we were broke, we never went without. Our income was cut by $45,000.00, but other than the damage to my credit rating, we lost nothing. It wasn't easy, but God brought us through

So there you have it. Now you should know why I couldn't comprehend what the Lord meant when He commanded me to be a help meet for my husband. I sincerely believed that I'd given up everything- my money, my career, my dreams and goals. I thought that there was nothing left to give. Yet there was. I gave up everything except the most vital thing of all, myself. I wanted to keep Fannie intact. So when the Lord called me to be a help meet for my husband and give up myself, I asked Him, "Why?" He gently told me, *"I need you to die to self, so that Pete can live."*

Now that I have enlightened you with my story, here are some examples of how a wife can be a help meet to her husband:

a. Prayer: The Greatest Asset

I have a secret. No, it's really not a secret. It's actually the truth, but it feels like a secret because many of us have not yet fully grasped its concept. What is the secret? Prayer. If it wasn't important to God, why did He speak of it so often in Scripture? Here are just a few examples:

Psalm 109:4, "For my love they are my adversaries: but I give myself unto prayer."

Psalm 141:2, " Let my prayer be set forth before thee as incense; and the lifting up of my hands as the evening sacrifice."

Psalm 143:1, "Hear my prayer, O Lord, give ear to my supplications: in thy faithfulness answer me, and in thy righteousness."

Proverbs 15:8, "The sacrifice of the wicked is an abomination to the Lord: but the prayer of the upright is his delight."

Proverbs 15:29, "The Lord is far from the wicked: but he heareth the prayer of the righteous."

Matthew 21:22, "And all things, whatsoever ye shall ask in prayer, believing, ye shall receive."

Philip. 4:6, "Be careful for nothing; but in every thing by prayer and supplication with thanksgiving let your requests be made known unto God."

Col. 4:2, "Continue in prayer, and watch in the same with thanksgiving;"

Interestingly enough, I received the revelation to pray for my husband one day as I watching an old television sitcom. To me, the shows from the fifties and sixties always made everything appear to be perfect. The mom was at home with the children and the house was always clean. She wore the perfect clothes—high heels and pearls, even in the daytime —just perfect. When her husband came home, she kissed him and dinner was always ready. No TV dinner, but a love labor-intensive meal followed by a mouth watering dessert. I yearned for this "perfect family" type of life that was portrayed on television: father, mother, daughter, son, and pet. I'd failed to realized that it was fake—an illusion. Make believe. It was only television. Unfortunately I modeled my perfect family based on what I saw on television and not the Word of God. My question to you is: what do you base yours on? (By the way, there are real families who are mirrored as these that are portrayed on television, but again, there is no "perfect" family, and life cannot be summed up in thirty minutes.)

It was during this period that the secret became revelation. The Lord showed me that cooking, cleaning, etc., are all responsibilities of being a wife. (Now remember, don't put yourself in bondage. How you perform your duties in your home is between you and your husband.) In general, they are just a part of the job description of a married woman. In the same way that the husband has a job description, so does the wife. The Lord showed me that we have it all wrong. Well not necessarily wrong, but we left out one crucial aspect of our responsibilities. Wives, we need to pray for our husbands. *And* I don't mean a simple cute prayer, such as, "Lord bless him and keep him." I mean, we need to really pray for him. Cover him with the Word of God and the Blood of Jesus. Pray for his health, his future, and his vision. These are our husbands, so it is imperative that we get down and dirty and pray for them.

For the most part, we have a handle on the cooking, the cleaning, raising our children, and supporting our men. They are instilled in us by every facet of life. And while they are relevant and necessary, it doesn't stop there. As wives we have unknowingly established the "learned behavior" of accepting our husbands as the men they are, and we assume that is how they always will be. Meaning they cannot change. (I'm referring to changing in a godly perspective). Well, if you take this attitude or notion, you are correct and your husband may never change. He may never become the man God created him to be. He may never reach his full potential in Christ—the reason why he was created, if you don't pray for him. Why? Because men, just like women, are the product of their upbringing and background. They will only get past those old things, and be healed and revived, as we pray it in. The real man in your husband may never come out because you failed to pray for him. Ouch! I know it hurts. Nevertheless this is what God showed me. If you pray for your husband, he may reach his destiny.

The Word clearly states in *Jeremiah 29:11 (NLT)*, *"For I know the plans I have for you," says the Lord. "They are plans for good and not for disaster, to give you a future and a hope."* When we are saved, we become new creatures. No longer are we products of our past. We begin the process of changing into what God has called us to be. Even if we never reach that potential on earth, in the spiritual realm we are changed. In the natural realm, this change doesn't happen instantly. It's a process that takes a lifetime. Every man has an appointed destiny that is ordained by God. What you see in your husband now, may not be the best God has for him. With that perspective in mind, we can say that there is a good, a better, and a best that God has to offer. And the Lord wants the best for your husband. When he is the best that he can be in the Lord, you will also fulfill your destiny.

The Lord tells us in Jeremiah 29:11, that He (Elohim, El-Shaddia, God) knows what's best for us. And why shouldn't He? He created us. He ordained purpose in us. Each of us was created for a purpose. Your husband has a destiny. It is your wifely duty and responsibility to pray for him to discover it. I want Pete to reach his fullest, his God-ordained destiny in Christ. Therefore, as his help meet, I must pray for him to get there.

As women of God, we must start praying for our husbands. I believe that it is a mandate from heaven. Yes, of course they want a good meal, clean clothes, a clean house, and a supportive wife. However, what they really need is for us to pray for them without ceasing. If you are too busy to pray for him, you need to rethink your priorities. You'll never know the outcome if you don't pray. He may already be successful in his chosen field, but wouldn't it be more of a blessing if he becomes successful in what God has ordained him to be? Which is better, God's path for your husband or the path your husband chose.

Stormie Omartian has a powerful book called, *"The Power of a Praying Wife."* I recommend that you read this book to get you started if you don't know how or what to pray. That is where I had to begin. Since then, I have learned to ask and depend on the Holy Spirit regarding how to pray for my husband. I would say, "Holy Spirit, you already know the plans God has for Pete. Tell me what to pray for him. Show me where my husband is having difficulties in his Christian walk." Then I would begin to pray according to what the Holy Spirit showed me. The Holy Spirit knows, so ask Him for direction. If your husband is having problems finding a job, pray, "Holy Spirit, you already know what he is supposed to do and where he is supposed to go. Open up the doors to make it happen." Be very specific when you pray.

I wish I could say I got this revelation right away, but you know my story. I was so busy trying to hold onto my identity and my life, while the enemy was trying to steal Pete's. Not physically, but he was trying to hinder him from reaching his destiny by using me. The Lord used to tell me, *"I can't work on Pete because I'm still trying to get you to submit. I am still trying to get you to die to self."*

You see, the issue was not about me at all. It was about my husband reaching his destiny in God. Pete had great things in store for him according to the plan of God, but that plan required me to decrease, submit, and pray for him. When I realized what I was doing, I stopped worrying about me and began to fight for my husband in prayer. There was more at stake and more people involved than just me. Here's something to ponder: If your husband doesn't reach his potential and his destiny, others may not reach theirs either.

One of the greatest gifts a help meet (wife) can give to her husband is to pray for him. Pray without ceasing for him. Pray for his areas of weaknesses, his strengths, his spiritual walk and his obedience to the Lord. Pray about his fears, his concerns, and his strongholds. Pray for his health, deliverance from satanic attacks, past failures and generational iniquities. Don't condemn, judge, or become frustrated with him, pray for him. If he is lazy, pray for him. If all he does is watch television, pray for him. You get the picture. Just pray.

Your husband doesn't need a new car, boat, or fishing reel. What he needs is for you to cover him with prayer. Those material things will come in their own time. Remember, you want the best for your husband, and so does God. Before you pray for others, pray for your husband. Intercessory prayer first begins with your husband.

b. Respect Your Husband

"So again I say, each man must love his wife as he loves himself, and the wife must respect her husband," Ephesians 5:33 (NLT)

Once again, while I was in church standing next to Pete, the Lord told me to treat Pete the way I treated my boss. (During that period, it seemed as if church was the only place the Lord would speak to me regarding how I treated my husband.) Me being me, said something like this, *"But my boss pays me a good salary."* (As you can imagine, my response didn't get very far with the Lord). The Lord informed me again, *"I want you to treat Pete like you treat your boss, and other authoritative figures. Help him reach his goals."* (Talk about long-suffering. The Lord was really long-suffering with me.)

Now before I go any further, let me say that I treat my husband very well. He deserves it. He is a good husband. However, that wasn't the case. I knew what the Lord was referring to. He was basically telling me that the same way I respected my boss as my head, or authority and assisted him in getting things done for the company, was the same way that I needed to treat my husband.

My former boss is the CEO at a healthcare facility where I used to work. Granted, in the beginning, we didn't get along very well. I remember a time when he told me he was the CEO and I was not. Anyway, in the third year of my employment, I became his executive assistant, which was one of the best jobs I have ever had. My job was to make sure that he was successful as a CEO. I remember him telling some board members and my husband at our annual board of director's banquet that I was his work wife. Professionally speaking that is. We all knew what he meant.

I believe that I was able to perform my job in an exemplary manner because I understood order from the military. He was the commander, and I was his executive assistant. He was the "Head", and I took great pleasure in making sure everything he needed was within his reach and taken care of. If it required me to work late, I did. Whatever it took to get the job accomplished, I was willing to do it. Did I sometimes feel overwhelmed? Yes. But I still did my job. Indeed, I was the consummate professional.

Each day, I made sure that I dressed and looked my best. I was not only representing me, I was representing my company and my boss. My hair was always groomed, and my attire was always professional and appropriate. Well, after five years, I left that job and started working for my husband. I was his office assistant for a manufacturing company that we own. Initially, I took on the same mannerisms and attitude as I did for my former boss. However, as time went by, I became slack in my appearance and professional attitude. After all, he was my husband. Why did I have to worry about my appearance or be professional?

There had been times at my previous job when I disagreed with my boss; and, when it was appropriate, I made suggestions. However, whether or not he received my suggestions, I didn't rebel. I always did what he asked, because that was my job. After all, I wasn't the one in charge. The vision wasn't mine. When I started working for my husband, if I thought he was making a bad decision I told him; unfortunately, not always in a nice manner. I also informed him that he should do it my way. Sadly, there were times when I didn't listen to him and just did it my way. Right or wrong, I overrode his authority, and I didn't respect his leadership.

Even though my way of doing things often proved best for the organization, I was still wrong. I wasn't the one in charge. I was getting paid for my expertise in administration, not for being the CEO. When I knew that he was making a bad decision, as an employee, I could have made tactful suggestions, but as his wife, I should have immediately started to pray. It took me a while to get this. Usually I would become frustrated, and although I did my job, I wasn't the happy camper. I whined and complained, instead of praying. And lo and behold, if I was correct, I couldn't wait to say, "I told you so." Sadly, I didn't respect him as my husband or my employer.

This brings us to the subject respecting your husband. I know what you're saying, *"But you don't know my husband."* No I don't, but I know my husband. Not to stereotype, but all men have some of the same characteristics and one is that they need to feel and be respected. Respect your husband as you would your boss, your pastor, or any other male figure in authority. When you are out in public, you are not only representing you, you are representing your husband. You may say, "This is me. This is who I am and how I dress." I am not trying to put you in bondage, but remember, in marriage, it's not just about you. There is more than one individual involved. Once you are married, it's about pleasing each other; and yes, sacrificing for each other. Let me ask you something, when you go on a job interview, or to any other place of importance, (i.e., a bank to request a loan), do you dress as if to say, "This is who I am so get over it?" Or do you dress to look as if you are trustworthy, responsible and reliable in order to get the loan or the job?

I am not suggesting that you dress like June Cleaver in "Leave it to Beaver." Neat and appropriate is all I'm saying. Believe me, if you practice this, you will feel better. And do not forget personal hygiene. Respect your husband enough to smell good for him. A couple of years ago my husband gave me the highest compliment. He told me that I was the cleanest person he knew and that I always smell nice. This was one of the highest compliments that I received as his wife, because it said to me that he noticed! But the truth is I wasn't just doing it for him. It's important for me as a woman to smell good, because it makes me feel good about myself. After a hard day, I shower, change, put on some body lotion and spray, slip into my clean pajamas, and feel like the woman God created me to be.

Not only must you respect your husband with your attitude and hygiene, but you must respect him with your lips. Remember, death and life are in the power of the tongue (Proverbs 18:21). You may not be aware of it, but we are all going to be judged for every idle word we speak (Matthew 12:36). So, if that's been you, simply repent and ask God for forgiveness (or as in my case, beg Him for forgiveness). Pray to the Holy Spirit to put a guard over your mouth, so that you won't say anything disrespectful to or about your husband. Also pray for your words to be seasoned with salt, and sweet as a honey comb. I am not asking you to be fake or phony. Rather, I am advising you to be careful of what you say, because nothing discourages a man more than hearing his wife (the love of his life), tell him that he is not doing a good job as a husband, provider, or father. He may hear this from others, but he doesn't need to hear it from you. And please, do not disrespect him in front of others, or out in public. When I hear a woman disrespecting her husband in public, I cringe and feel sorry for that man. She may feel that she has every right to do so, but she doesn't. What she fails to understand is that she is attacking and stripping him of his confidence, and showing disrespect towards the order of God. Once again, this is where prayer comes into play.

I don't care how angry I am with Pete, I do my best not to show disrespect for him in front of others. Now, I have not always been here, but I am very cautious of this. In the past when I did slip, which I'll share later, when I realized what I'd done, I repented and asked Pete and the Lord to forgive me.

In the same way, it's just as important that you don't allow others to speak or act disrespectfully towards your husband. I don't care if he has a substance abuse problem, or other visible flaws. Do not allow others to disrespect him, not even in a joking manner. That is one of the lessons I learned while writing this book. I never allow people to talk about my husband; but, in the past in my frustration with him, I would tell a family member or a very close and spiritually mature friend, of my feelings. I was wrong. It's okay to go to mature saints and inform them that you are having problems within the marriage, or with your husband. But it is not okay that you start belittling your husband, causing them to possibly take sides or to have a negative perception of him. (By the way, Pete usually wasn't the problem. It was me.)

I'll never forget one event in particular when the Lord really showed me how wrong it was to disrespect my husband in front of others. On this particular day, Pete had made me very angry. (Remember I was dying to self, so everything was making me angry). Well that day, we were having dinner with another couple. In the midst of the conversation, Pete said something that was obviously wrong, and the three of us knew that he was wrong. At that moment, I had the choice to pray for the Lord to put a guard over my mouth, or when I would speak for my words to be as sweet as honey. I didn't do either. In my frustration, I spoke my mind. I disrespected him in front of the couple, and it was very obvious. Nevertheless, I believed I was right, so I didn't care about his feelings.

That evening I went to church without Pete. (He had to take care of some business at the shop). After service, I looked for the man who we had dined with earlier and once I saw him, I began to engage in a conversation with him. In honesty, I wanted to gloat about me being right. I wanted him to take my side. But from the beginning, he gently put me in my place and informed me that even though I was correct, my mistake was in taking sides against my husband and causing dissension. He also told me that he loved Pete, and that Pete was a man of God; so, he wasn't going to talk about him for my benefit or to justify me being right. Ouch! I didn't realize what I had done until two days later. I repented to the Lord and asked for forgiveness. I also asked Pete for forgiveness. (During my dying to self process I repented a lot.)

When I say this was a rare occasion, I am being honest. I love my husband and believe that he is the greatest man on earth. But you see how the enemy crept in? Whether or not Pete was right or wrong, I had no right to disrespect him. I learned a major lesson. My hus band is a man of God; therefore, I need to respect him as such. We as women need to be very careful how we talk about our husbands to others. I am not saying that you cannot go to a mature spiritual friend, (I emphasize the word *mature*) to talk about things pertaining to your husband. Talk, but do not complain. That person shouldn't need to take sides with you against your husband. She or he is there to listen and give you the Word of God, or provide sound doctrinal advice to aid you in addressing and hopefully rectifying the problem-- nothing more, nothing less. Anything else is contrary to the Word of God.

As soldiers in the military, we are taught and trained to respect leadership, all the way up to the President of the United States. I find it interesting to realize how I still live by this code. But the Lord showed me the sad truth. Subconsciously, I had more respect for others in authority than I did for my own husband, who is actually the second most important person in my life after the Lord. My husband, your husband, whether we care to admit it or not, is the second person in the chain of command. Your husband, while not perfect, is a man of God who deserves your respect. You are to respect and appreciate him like you do others in authority.

c. Vision and Purpose

It's funny how our generation of women assumes that nothing will change when we get married. Sure there will be adjustments to make, but overall we believe that everything will remain the same. You know the drill. The husband has his agenda and the wife has hers. There will be compromises; however, the compromises will not alter their personal agendas. But in truth, when it comes to marriage, the only real agenda is God's. There are no compromises with God's plan for the marriage.

Before I ever thought of getting married again, the Lord gave me a scripture, which today is still embedded in my heart: *"Wives fit into your husband plans...," 1 Peter 3:1" (The Living Bible).* Initially, I didn't fully understand what He was trying to tell me. As I said before, I assumed I was fitting into Pete's plans by cooking, cleaning, taking care of our home and being intimate. Yet, in all of this, I still had my own plans. Even when I got out of the military, I still had my own agenda.

It was a couple of years ago the Lord opened my eyes to a greater revelation regarding my marriage. This has helped me tremendously to live out my role as a help meet for my husband. The revelation is this: The husband has the vision for the marriage, and although the wife has a godly vision, in the marriage she humbly sets aside her vision and submits to the vision of her husband. What I am saying? The vision of the house is not yours; it's your husbands. In Habbakkak 2:2 it states, *"Write the vision down."* It also states in Proverbs 29:18 KJV, *"My people perish because of no vision."* How about this,

"And Jesus knew their thoughts, and said unto them, Every kingdom divided against itself is brought to desolation; and every city or house divided against itself shall not stand," Matthew 12:25.

The order of God is the husband, then the wife. Not the other way around. Therefore, since this is God's divine order, to whom do you think He will give the vision of the house to? Why the Head of the household, of course, which is the husband. If both the husband and the wife vie to receive visions from the Lord, the house and the marriage will become a state of confusion. It will not stand due to the mere fact that each one will be trying to accomplish his vision apart from the other.

Like it or not, when we get married, we have to fit into our husband's plans. As women, the minute we say "I do," we are saying before people and the Lord that we are agreeing to accommodate our husband's plans. For that reason, I explicitly inform ladies to do all that they are called to do and be before they get married, because in order for a marriage to work, you must fit into the vision God gave the man. Don't rush into marriage if you are not ready to make such a sacrifice.

When I met Pete, first of all I didn't go to him, he came to me. The Bible says *"The man that finds a wife finds a good thing,"* Proverbs 18:22. Pete was ready for a wife. During this time the Lord was preparing me to be a wife. (Although at the time I didn't know it.) When Pete came looking for me, I was ready to be found. During my waiting period, the Lord was purging me both spiritually and physically. One way he was doing this was by showing me specific scriptures pertaining to the role of a wife. Also, during that period, the only people I had contact with outside of my job were Christian couples, especially married Christian women.

Before that time, I rarely liked to do girly things. I was a soldier, and the only women I associated with were also soldiers. My conversations consisted of military, politics, and world matters. After the military, I wanted to be a lawyer and a politician. In fact, when I met Pete, I was studying for my LSAT. When Pete asked for my hand in marriage, I immediately said yes. Before the big day, because the courtship whirlwind only took three weeks, I sought counseling and prayed to the Lord for clarity on whether or not Pete was my husband. One of my prayers was, "Lord if he is not my husband, get him out of my life immediately." Well, you know the outcome; however, even as we planned to marry, I had no intention of giving up my plans to go to law school.

As we planned the wedding, all the way up to the actual day, and even after all these years of marriage, the scripture, *"Wives fit into your husband's plans"* has never left me. Every time I tried to do things my way, this particular scripture came to my mind. You know my story. It was hard for me. I was a product of the nineties, an era where independent women were the norm. Remember the mottos of those years? "I'm every woman. Hear me roar. I'm invincible. I am woman. I don't need a man. I can do anything a man can do, but better." This was, and still is, my generation's train of thought. We all wanted to accomplish something great— be someone great. We all had our individual vision. This is probably why it's easier for us to accept the world's ideology on this subject rather than God's.

If your husband does not have a vision for the house, or you don't know what it is, ask him. If he doesn't know, pray for him. Pray that God will reveal it to him, because the vision involves both your destiny and his. I used to ask Pete about the vision for our family. When he didn't produce it, I began to pray. Now we have vision. It is very important that your husband has a vision. Without a vision, he is doing you and your family an injustice.

Now as a wife, don't think at all the Lord has forgotten you or abandoned you. You may not have the vision for the house, but you do have a purpose. And your purpose is equally significant for the vision to manifest. In fact, the vision needs your purpose to fulfill or complete it. It states in Jeremiah 1:5, *"Before you were formed in your mother's womb, I knew you, you are marvelously made."* And in Jeremiah 29:11 it says, *"I know the plans I have for you...."* You see, these scriptures clearly depict Jesus' plans for you. Not your husband, not your kids, but you. My purpose coincides with the vision the Lord gave Pete. Pete is called to be in ministry. I am called to be his wife. And while I am still his wife, assisting him in what God has called him to do; I am fulfilling my own personal calling. I am writing to and for women, ministering to them alongside my husband, doing exactly what I was created to do, and fulfilling my purpose. What a joy. All because I was able to fit into my husband's plans (vision).

I am not stressed out like I used to be, because now I have the grace from God to do my assignment. In the past, women have asked me if I was happy. Some even said I was crazy for giving up a successful career to follow a man. They would ask, "What if he left you, then what?" This question more than any other distressed me, especially since that was what happened in my previous marriage. It took me a long time to overcome this fear. But through tests, trials, and tribulations, I learned to trust and lean on Jesus. I relied on the Word of God to overcome the thought of Pete leaving me. Now I am more secure in knowing God's got my back. He wouldn't ask me to do something contrary to His plans for me.

When I got the revelation in my spirit that the man has the vision and that I have a purpose, it quickened me to pray intensely for my husband. I would tell him, "Pete my destiny is in you being what God called you to be. When you are what God called you to be, I am what the Lord created me to be. Your husband may not be a go-getter and perhaps he doesn't have a vision for your home. Tell the Lord about it as I did. I would say, *"Lord I know you gave me this husband, but I cannot be what you called me to be, if he is not doing what you called him to do. He is the head, and I am not going to go against your divine order. You have to fix it. You have to fix Pete."*

I went to the Lord about it, and He took care of it. Now I am fulfilling my purpose and assignment. My assignment is to pray for my husband so that he can get to where he needs to be in God. I don't know what your assignment is; however, I do know that God does not go against His order. When I finally started to really pray for my husband, not only did things begin to turn around, but Pete also started changing. The vision was becoming a reality.

There is an exception to this rule. Please know that I am not telling you to go against your husband at any time. But if he is not lis tening to God, there may be occasions when you have to take the lead until he gets back on track. But always remember, you must still respect him. For instance, when Moses neglected to perform a circumcision, his wife went before him and did it. She furiously told him that he was about to get them killed for not doing as God commanded. It was obvious, she had heard from God; therefore, she was in order. (Please read Exodus 4: 24-26 for further clarity.)

On these occasions, before you take the lead in the household you better make sure you are hearing from God, and not you or anyone else for that matter. You can do more harm than good. And remember, this is not a permanent position. It's temporary. When your husband is ready to accept his role and position, cheerfully relinquish it to him. If not, it will cause much tension and friction in the marriage.

d. Stand by Your Man

Country Singer Tammy Wynette sang the famous song *"Stand by Your Man."* I never really listened to the entirety of the song. In honesty, I only know this one verse, "Stand by Your Man." And that is what we are going to talk about now. A help meet stands by her man of God, regardless, during the good, the bad, and the downright turbulence.

It was while I was in the process of writing this book the concept of standing by your man became real to me. Before I go on, let me reiterate one thing. When we are referring to standing by your man, we are talking about God-fearing men, who are walking right with God. If your husband is doing something contrary to the Word of God, or against the law, you are not to stand by him. You must pray for him, but do not adhere to his wrongdoings, or follow him as he walks in sin.

Standing by your man was the one test I had to endure throughout my first years of marriage. In fact, while writing this book, this was one of my tests I had to undergo or take several times. Could I stand by my man? As you have read, I had been taking this test for many years, because I had never passed. I'd missed one or two subjects, which caused me to go back to remedial training, (I went through a lot of remedial training during my dying to self). Hallelujah, this time I finally passed the test.

God was calling my husband to start a new journey in his life or walk with Him. Much like Abram and Sara, we were to go into foreign territory. We had just left a ministry we loved. For ten years this ministry was our home and the people were our family. Being far away from our places of birth and real families (Pete is from Detroit and I am from Baltimore), and traveling so much in the military, the thought of uprooting and getting out of our comfort zone was not pleasing to us, especially at our age. But Pete heard from God, so he had to obey.

We were not going far, but because of the distance, we had to put our home on the market to sell, and went in search of a new home in the new ministry location. That doesn't sound hard, (and maybe it wouldn't have been for others), but it was for us. We were about to go to a place—the wilderness, where it would take God and only God to bring us out. I was about to understand what the concept of dying to flesh really meant.

We met an individual who wanted to buy the house. We had prayed, "Lord send someone who really needs a home." So when she came, we both felt that she was the one. Now looking back, I can say that the obstacles in the process were not about the house, they were about the purging of self.

Perhaps you may think we were crazy, but because we believed this woman was the one, we made the decision to move out of our home and into our place of business, allowing her to move in before we closed on the house. Well, we didn't close as expected. So there we were, me, my husband and our dog (a 120 pounds Rottweiler named T-Bone), living within the compounds of our company. The living quarters were not bad. We had a full bathroom with a shower, a full kitchen and plenty of room; it was just not what we were used to. (One advantage for me was that I was able to get some much needed work done for the company.)

Because of the new mortgage rules, we were unable to close on the house as planned, which meant we couldn't purchase a new home. You may be thinking, *"Wait a minute. You moved out of your home, allowed someone else to move in before you closed, moved into your place of business, and you don't think this was foolish?"* To the majority, it probably looks and is foolish, but we never know what God plans for us and how it will manifest. The Word clearly states in 1st Corinthians, *"For the wisdom of this world is foolishness with God. For it is written, He taketh the wise in their own craftiness."* And by the way, we lived at the shop for over a month, while still paying all the utilities and mortgage at the house; after all, it was still our house.

Although the decision was ours, I believe it was the leading of the Lord that took us there. Because it was in that place, we were able to see God in a different perspective. It was there that we learned to trust Him on a deeper level like never before. We didn't know what was going on. We had honestly thought it would be easy to sell our house and buy another. What we didn't realize was that the enemy was trying to distract us, and possibly even destroy our marriage.

I won't go into details, but this period was one of the hardest of my Christian walk; and yet, it was also my breakthrough. It was in that place I truly learned to be a help meet to my husband. It was there that we became not only one in marriage, but one in the Spirit of the Lord. It was there in that place the Lord would allow me to go through a trial that I don't wish on another. The Lord kept me isolated from all of my friends. I couldn't tell them or explain what was happening for the mere fact I didn't know what was going on. For the first time in my marriage, I had to totally depend on Pete. And he was depending on God because he didn't know what was happening either. We had to live on blind faith. As you can imagine, being classified as a "Type A" personality, I literally thought I was losing my mind. Things were so far out of my control. Still trying to figure things out, I called two of my mature Christian friends from my former church in Texas. And while their prayers were comforting, they were not enough. What I failed to understand was that in our wilderness place, no one could help us but the Lord.

By the fourth week of living at the company, I had finally made up my mind. I said, "Lord I surrender." At that moment, I fell to the floor, groaning and crying out to the Lord. With tears streaming down my face and neck, I begged for forgiveness, while repenting and yielding to Him. I had enough. I didn't want to continue to live for Fannie- for self anymore. I didn't want to be in control anymore. I didn't want to put my husband through any more turmoil because I couldn't submit. I wanted God and His will. I needed Him, His peace, and most importantly, I needed His presence.

Both Pete and I had to come to this place, isolated from everyone;

a wilderness experience that brought us to our knees, breaking both of us so that we could be what God needed us to be for each other and for Him. From that day on, Pete started making the decisions, as I yielded and allowed him to be the head of our home. From that day on, I offered suggestions or provided pertinent input, but in the end I respected his right to make the final decision. It was during this time I had accepted my assignment and fervently began to pray for my husband. I finally allowed Pete to take the lead in the home, and in the process I found a peace I had never known.

While all of this was taking place, two major things happened and we had to make some major decisions pertaining to the house. One decision, Pete had to make while I was out. When I came in, I could see in his face that he was a little upset. He told me about the decision he had made in my absence. I didn't say anything because on my way home I was praying for him. I wrapped my arms around him to assure him that I was in agreement. He breathed a sign of relief. In the past, I had always questioned or argued with him about his decision. He assumed that I would do likewise this time. That night he told me something that was like a sweet melody to my ears. He told me that he needed me. I was his help meet. Now he said he told me this before, but I can't remember. But that night, I knew the house was in order. Finally, we were in alignment with God.

The next day, we had to make another decision pertaining to the house. As hard as it was for me, I didn't say a word. Again, I had already prayed for God's will to be done, and for Pete to make the proper decision. However, I did tell him that whatever he decided, I had his back. With that in mind, he made the decision, and everything worked out fine. You see, I had already made up in my mind, I was going to let Pete be the husband and I was going to be the wife. I was going to stand by him, through the good, the bad, the trials, the tribulations, the crisis, whatever. I was going to be his cheerleader. Later that same day, Pete once again blessed me by saying that although the decision had been hard to make, I had made it easier because I had supported him. He also said it means everything for husbands to know that their wives will stand by and with them when they have tough decisions to make.

Will Pete ever make unwise decisions? Yes. He is not perfect. Will I continue to stand with him, whether the decision is good or bad once he has made it? Yes. You see, I have something powerful in my corner. I have a relationship with the Lord. I can pray to the Lord on Pete's behalf for him to make the correct decisions. And if he doesn't, I can pray for mercy, or for the Lord to fix the wrong.

Ladies, I am not saying to be a doormat, or to be passive and agree with everything your husband says (without providing positive feedback). Marriage is based on compromise. In a good marriage, decisions are mutual—give and take. Nevertheless, the husband has the final say.

The day I was called a help meet by my husband was truly a day of victory. It was a major breakthrough. I was standing by my man, and more significantly, my Lord and Savior, Jesus Christ was pleased.

e. Love Your Man

"Though I speak with the tongues of men and of angels, and have not charity, I am become as sounding brass, or a tinkling cymbal. [2] And though I have the gift of prophecy, and understand all mysteries, and all knowledge; and though I have all faith, so that I could remove mountains, and have not charity, I am nothing. [3] And though I bestow all my goods to feed the poor, and though I give my body to be burned, and have not charity, it profiteth me nothing. [4] Charity suffereth long, and is kind; charity envieth not; charity vaunteth not itself, is not puffed up, [5] Doth not behave itself unseemly, seeketh not her own, is not easily provoked, thinketh no evil; [6] Rejoiceth not in iniquity, but rejoiceth in the truth; [7] Beareth all things, believeth all things, hopeth all things, endureth all things. [8] Charity never faileth: but whether there be prophecies, they shall fail; whether there be tongues, they shall cease; whether there be knowledge, it shall vanish away. [9] For we know in part, and we prophesy in part. [10] But when that which is perfect is come, then that which is in part shall be done away. [11] When I was a child, I spake as a child, I understood as a child, I thought as a child: but when I became a man, I put away childish things. [12] For now we see through a glass, darkly; but then face to face: now I know in part; but then shall I know even as also I am known. [13] And now abideth faith, hope, charity, these three; but the greatest of these is charity (LOVE)" 1 Corithians13:1-13.

About ten years ago, I was reading an article in a Christian magazine. In the article, a woman was sharing her testimony of how her husband was so mean and cruel to her, she didn't know what to do. She wasn't led to divorce him, but instead to pray for him. In the midst of praying for husband, the Lord told her to exceptionally love her husband, regardless of how he treated her. In one incident, her husband wanted a glass of lemonade. His request was demanding and very rude, but she obeyed the Lord and lovingly gave him the glass of lemonade. The end result was that after years, her husband not only became gentle and loving, he became a powerful man of God. Her obedience to love her husband in spite of his actions paid off. I wish I would have gotten this when I first read this article, but it would take me ten years to finally get this revelation.

In Matthew 22:37- 40 the disciples asked Jesus, which was the greatest commandment in the law. His reply was, *"[37] Thou shalt love the Lord thy God with all thy heart, and with all thy soul, and with all thy mind. [38] This is the first and great commandment. [39] And the second is like unto it, Thou shalt love thy neighbour as thyself. [40] On these two commandments hang all the law and the prophets."*

The first and greatest commandment is to love God with all our heart, soul, and mind. The second is to love our neighbor as we would ourselves. This is what I want to focus on now, loving others as we love ourselves.

Love is not selfish. It is not jealous; it is not envious, and it is not puffed up, nor is it vain. Love is longsuffering- thank God! It is forgiving and merciful, it rejoices in the truth, it never fails, and it bears all things, good and bad. Love doesn't take sides—"What good if I have everything else going for me, but I don't love my neighbor as I love myself," I Corinthians 13.

As a help meet, it is important that you not only stand by your husband and respect him, but you love him. Regardless of how he treats you, you must still respond with love and respect in order for God to grab hold of his heart. Is this hard? Yes, often times it is. Do we sometimes fail at this? Yes, many times we do. But, regardless of how Pete treats me, whether intentionally or unintentionally, I still have to love and respect him. I have to love him the same way I want him to love me, and the way that I love myself.

For the past ten years, God has loved me in spite of my rebellion and disobedience. He was very patient, very gentle, and extremely longsuffering with me just like He was patient and longsuffering with the children of Israel. Over and over the Lord told them what was required of them to get His blessings, and over and over they did the opposite. I was no different. Like the Israelites, the Lord, told me what I needed to do, and I did the opposite. I thank God that in my quest to keep my will, He didn't give up on me. He continued to love me. Even today, with all of my issues, He loves me.

I can recall during one New Years' Eve service my Pastor at our former church had people give their testimonies regarding the previous year's blessings. Many people were thankful for their health, new jobs, new homes, and new babies (all appropriate things for which to give thanks). Though I didn't give my testimony, in my heart I was thankful that I was still alive. I am serious! On that new day in a new year, I was thankful the Lord had allowed me to live another year in spite of my rebellion and disobedience. I was thankful for His mercy, grace and forgiveness. With tears running down my cheeks, that year I knew He loved me enough to preserve me. That's love!

Many of us would have thrown in the towel, or probably wanted a divorce if the Lord had told us to love our husbands like He'd told the woman in the magazine article. I know there were times I too wanted to throw in the towel with my marriage. Being truthful, there were even times I wanted to actually throw the towel at Pete, and possibly put something hard in it so he could feel the impact. But two things stopped me. I love the Lord too much, and I love my husband.

You see, because the Lord is merciful, forgiving and very long-suffering with me, I had to extend those same qualities to Pete. If I wanted him to love me like I needed and wanted to be loved, I had to love him the same way. Scriptures tells us to do unto others as we want others to do unto us. If I want respect, forgiveness, mercy, fairness, longsuffering and patience from others, I have to give these qualities. If I want to be caressed, pampered, joked with, smiled upon, nurtured, etc., I have to provide these things to Pete and to others. I hate negativity, phoniness, gossip, and being hurtful to others. You guessed it… I have to display characteristics that are opposite to those.

This is all a part of loving and treating others as you want others to love and treat you. If you want your husband to respect you, then you have to respect your husband. If you want your husband to

say kind things to you, then you must speak kind words to him and about him. If you don't want your husband to be cruel or to say nasty words to you, don't speak cruel or nasty words to him. Love him as you love yourself. Treat him as you want to be treated. When you are able to love others as you would yourself, you are on your way to mastering the greatest commandment of all, "*Thou shalt love the Lord thy God with all thy heart, and with all thy soul, and with all thy mind,*" Matthew 22:37. By the way, the Lord will teach you how to love your husband. Just rely on him and His wisdom to show you.

Section 2. Some Characteristics of a Help Meet

After many years, I still cannot forget the lasting impression one particular woman made on me. I don't recall her name; however, her eloquence as a woman of God has never left my spirit. Her impact still penetrates my heart today. If ever there was a woman I longed to be, she is the one. Although she was my age, her wisdom and stature as a woman far surpassed mine. And though she was the employee I had hired, it was she who taught me. Her demeanor was different than that of anyone I'd ever met. She had a gentle and calm spirit, and I loved talking to her about the things of God. Her words were soothing to my soul. Not only did I admire her, but I looked up to her. I longed to possess the same womanly qualities she had acquired. She was beautiful externally, yet her internal beauty surpassed the outer. She radiated the fragrance of the Lord's presence. She possessed something I wanted in my own life—to be a woman after God's own heart.

While reading "*A Woman After God's Own Heart,*" by author Elizabeth George for the second time (the first time I read it, I thought it was a little too far-fetched. In my defense, I had just started the process of dying to self, so nothing was making sense to me), there was a segment of the book which stated that I should plan for my husband daily; treat him as if the king had just come home from battle. Well this didn't go well with my spirit, so I laid the book down and said out loud, "Yeah Right!" Later that night, I was writing down some notes for this book. Guided by the Holy Spirit, I was just writing away, not bothering to read what I was writing. After I finished, (which took about two hours), I started reading what I had written, and immediately began to laugh. The Lord had rebuked me in such a way that I didn't see it coming. Although I didn't use the same words Mrs. George had, I had said essentially the same thing: Treat your husband like a king. As far-fetched as it sounds (and many women like me, in the beginning, cannot see or don't want to see), this is vital to the success of the marriage. Look at it this way, if you want your husband to treat you like the queen you are, treat him like the king he is.

Here are some characteristics of a help meet I have found helpful through my reading and, of course by the guidance of the Holy Spirit. I will not go to great lengths on each, but I will just touch on them for illumination purposes. I hope they will assist you in being a help meet to your husband.

1. **Keep God First**: God is first and foremost, no exceptions. If you allow anyone, including your husband, to come before the Lord, you have already lost the battle. It is imperative that as women first, wives second, mothers third, we seek the Lord. Early in the morning, noonday, and evening, seek His face and get into His presence. Never get too busy to spend time with Jesus.

2. **Know Yourself and Your Purpose**: If you do not know yourself and your purpose, you can get lost in the process of being a help meet to your husband. Know your general make-up: your strengths, your weaknesses, your desires and your fears. Many women think that after they get married their only purpose is to serve their husband. Remember, while your husband has the vision, you have a purpose. Fulfilling your purpose will keep you from losing your identity.

3. **Maintain Your Individuality In God**: The Lord created you. Never forget this or allow anyone to change you into what they want you to become. If change is needed you will know, but more importantly the Lord will know. He will change you as necessary. If anyone tries to change you into something the Lord has not ordained or called you to be, run quickly in the opposite direction. Your laughter, personality, and make-up are one of a kind and designed by God. And though you will become more refined as you die to self, you will not be changed to the point where you will become someone else. Maintaining your identity will enable your husband to become the man he needs to be.

4. **Take Care of Your Husband's Needs**: Prepare for him daily, pray for him, and praise him. His needs are not only physical (such as

cooking, cleaning, and intimacy), but he also has spiritual needs. Treat him as if he is the most important person in your world other than Jesus. Treat him like a king because the everyday stress of being a man can cause him to falter or become disillusioned. He is the provider; however, sometimes, he needs you to provide for him. (This includes sexually too, as studies have shown that sex is a real stress reliever).

5. **Take Care of His Intimate Needs**: Whether you want to believe it or not, your body does not belong to you. It belongs to your husband, and his body belongs to you.

The wife hath not power of her own body, but the husband: and likewise also the husband hath not power of his own body, but the wife," 1 Corinthians 7:4 (KJV).

Do not deprive your husband of sex. Due to the very nature of being a woman, there will be times when you cannot engage in sex; however, do not go for long periods of time without sexually satisfying him. And let me warn you, if you are punishing him by withholding sex, you are operating in the spirit of witchcraft. If there are times that you do not feel like it, pray to the Lord for strength to satisfy and please your husband. This is what I do. Not only does the Lord give me strength, but He gives me supernatural power so that both my husband and I are pleased.

If your husband had a hard day, or is really bothered about something, on these occasions, don't wait on him, seduce him. Sometimes when he comes home tired, before dinner is made, get intimate with him. Rock his world! (You have to be real, because the enemy is real. So if I offend you, be offended, but just do it).

Also, get to know what pleases your husband- what turns him on. Don't look to the world in books, magazines, or talk shows. If you really want to know how to please your husband, ask the Holy Spirit. You'll be surprised at what He may tell you. Intimacy is a spiritual thing, not a worldly thing; therefore, inquire about it to the One who created it. Contrary to popular opinion, your husband doesn't want a Delilah (or any other woman) in his bedroom. Don't believe this lie from the enemy. He wants you (his wife) in the bedroom that you both share.

6. **Know Where Your Husband Is Financially**: You promised to keep him for richer or poorer, for good or bad, and in sickness and health. So in regards to finances, do not try to keep up with the Joneses' because they are perpetually broke. If you can't shop for new clothes, keep the ones you have clean and presentable. If you can't afford new outfits, find inexpensive accessories to change your look. When we were searching for a home, we were approved for a large amount. We had found a home that was everything we wanted. But after praying to the Lord regarding whether or not we should purchase it, we decided that at the time it was too much money to invest in a home. We knew where we were financially. If we would have purchased the home, it would have set us back tremendously. We would have been house rich, but money poor—financially struggling. We didn't feel like keeping up with the *Joneses'*.

7. **Assist Your husband Financially**: According to God's Word, the husband is the provider, but there are still times when he needs his help meet to assist him financially and keep financial matters in perspective. If it is not in the budget, it's not in the budget. If he is doing his best at the present time, assist him. Do not badger him with your complaints on what you do not have, instead pray about the matter. God can and will take care of your financial problems if you bow your heart to His leading. Finally, if you have to get a job, get a job- need I say more.

8. **Prioritize Your Time/ Time Management**: Eliminate idleness and procrastination by prioritizing your time and learning to say no. While writing this book, I couldn't allow myself to become distracted by telephone calls or last minute invitations. I was on a mission from the Lord. Other than my husband (because your wifely and motherly duties come first before anything else), this was my first priority. Do

not allow anyone, not even your family, ministry or your job to put you into bondage or take you away from what you need to do. For example, if you are too busy doing ministry, taking care of others, or even working late, there is a strong possibility that you are neglecting your own family and home. My oldest sister, April, is a prime example. She does not let anyone or anything come before her husband or children (in that order).

To eliminate idleness and procrastination, time yourself on the internet, on the phone, and while watching television. Set limits and stick to them. If you are watching television, do something productive at the same time. I had a problem with playing games on my computer for hours at a time, and I actually had to wean myself from this. The key is discipline.

9. **Determine What You Want In Your House**: Once again, my sister April enlightened me on this. She always keeps her home neat and orderly. When asked how she manages to do this, she said that she always wants peace in her home; so, this is what she strives for, and she has succeeded. She doesn't allow anything or anyone to disrupt her peaceful sanctuary. As for me, I not only want peace, but I want the presence of the Lord permeated throughout my home, so I work to make that happen. Decide what kind of atmosphere you want in your home, and do what you have to do to make it happen.

10. **Maintain Your House**: Keep it clean and orderly. Whether it seems fair or not, your home is a reflection of the woman who lives there. It doesn't have to be picture perfect or spotless, just neat and orderly. If your home is always messy, then you may be too busy. Stop and take an inventory. Get a maid if you have to. Prioritize your time and organize your home, because while he may tolerate it your husband doesn't really want to come home to a chaotic and cluttered house. A cleaner, more organized home creates an atmosphere that is warm and cozy. So what your furniture is outdated? Keep it clean and neat. Buy slipcovers for a new look. Real friends don't look at what you do or don't have. Only superficial people do that. Another important thing is to make sure everything is in its place. Find a place to put

away the children's toys so that they don't take over the house. Train your children early, especially your sons, to pick up after themselves. It will pay dividends in their future and their wives will thank you.

11. Maintain your appearance: You may not have the latest designer clothes, but this doesn't negate the necessity to maintain your appearance. We didn't have a washing machine growing up, but we had soap. I used to wash my clothes in the kitchen sink with Ivory Soap. No one outside of our family knew. They only knew I was always clean and neat. (That was when I became a teenager, because as a child, I was a dirt bag.) Don't just maintain your appearance for your husband, do it for yourself. You are a King's daughter, therefore you represent Jesus.

Perhaps you are slipping in your appearance because you have gained weight. Well, so have the rest of us. I used to be twenty pounds lighter. I can fix the problem, but I cannot worry about it. I have the choice. The key is to dress in styles that flatter your figure. And once again, be neat and clean in your appearance. It's good for your confidence.

12. Listen More and Speak Less: *(James 1:19)* (This is a point I am definitely working on.) Have you ever called someone but you didn't want their advice? All you wanted was for them to listen while you spoke. What if the person continues interrupting you, never permitting you the chance to convey what's really on your mind? After a while you hang up with the person and say to yourself, "Boy she/he doesn't let you talk." That was me. I was the person who went on and on, talking instead of listening. Now I am learning to listen more and talk less. I know I have the gift of gab, but now I am learning when to open up my gift. And you know what? By listening, I am seeing more and obtaining more wisdom. A wise woman once told me, you can always tell what a person is really like by allowing them to speak (because oftentimes, people are really not about what they speak about).

Also, be careful what you listen to. Do not let others pollute your thoughts with gossip or vile speech. Guard your heart (Proverbs 4:23).

Eliminate your exposure to things that don't glorify God.

13. **Manage Your Money:** You have the job you wanted, making plenty of money, yet you are in debt up to your knees. You are driving an expensive, beautiful, state of the art car, but you don't have car or health insurance. You are wearing the latest style of clothes: Prada, Gucci, and Coach-- even the movie stars don't dress as well as you do; yet, you are still wondering and praying about how to pay for your child's college education. You are "living large" in a beautiful home that's in a well-established neighborhood, but you don't have the money to pay for your utilities, or worse buy food. Need I say more?

The money you are spending doesn't belong to you. It belongs to the Lord for the building of His Kingdom; not for building up the world. I am not saying He doesn't want you to have fine things. He does. After all, you are a King's child. What I am saying is that you need to keep everything in perspective and balance. Don't pray for a miracle about a certain bill that needs to be paid, when you are not a tither and you spent your money on clothes. You better pray for mercy. I know I wasn't a good steward of my money. I gave so much money to the mall and other department stores; I'm not exaggerating when I say that I could have put someone through college. It took me a long time to get delivered, but my need to shop is dwindling down. I am learning to manage my money, or should I say God's money.

In managing money, first things first: give your tithes, give offerings, get out of debt, pay yourself, and plan for retirement. If you don't know how to plan accordingly, get professional help. Like I said, I gave all of my money to department stores by buying material items that I threw away a long time ago. I wished I would have been more diligent with the money the Lord entrusted to me. If I had, I would be so far ahead of the game.

Now that I have discussed what it means to be a help meet to your husband, let's discuss about being a hindrance. You will be surprised how many of us are, yet we don't know it. I know I was.

Chapter 4

Are You A Hindrance To Your Husband?

Before we discuss being a hindrance, let me define what a hindrance is: The definition of hindrance is a thing that provides resistance, delay, or obstruction to someone or something. It hurts instead of helps or assists- it interrupts or delays an action or a purpose. Now lets discuss how we as wives can hinder our husbands and the overall marriage. Let us begin with the first wife Eve.

Section 1. Eve: The First Wife

"Now the serpent was more subtle than any beast of the field which the Lord God had made. And he said unto the woman, Yea, hath God said, Ye shall not eat of every tree of the garden? [2] And the woman said unto the serpent, We may eat of the fruit of the trees of the garden: [3] But of the fruit of the tree which is in the midst of the garden, God hath said, Ye shall not eat of it, neither shall ye touch it, lest ye die. [4] And the serpent said unto the woman, Ye shall not surely die: [5] For God doth know that in the day ye eat thereof, then your eyes shall be opened, and ye shall be as gods, knowing good and evil. [6] And when the woman saw that the tree was good for food, and that it was pleasant to the eyes, and a tree to be desired to make one wise, she took of the fruit thereof, and did eat....," Genesis 3:1-6.

And the Lord God said unto the woman, "What is this that thou hast done?" And the woman said, "The serpent beguiled me, and I did eat," Genesis 3:13.

"Unto the woman he said, I will greatly multiply thy sorrow and thy

conception; in sorrow thou shalt bring forth children; and thy desire shall be to thy husband, and he shall rule over thee," Genesis 3:16.

Like so many of us today, Eve allowed someone, or in her case the serpent, to deceive her into thinking that she was not the woman God created her to be, when in truth she was. When she took a bite of the fruit, three major things came into place: (1) She lost her identity- she no longer knew who she was, (2) She no longer understood her purpose or why she was created, and lastly, (3) She lost the ability to have intimate fellowship with God (which to me was the most devastating of the three).

Before the fall, Eve knew who she was. She was Adam's help meet. This was who God created her to be. She was bone of Adam's bone and flesh of his flesh. She didn't have to compete with him and he didn't have to compete with her. She didn't have to dispute over the order God had ordained. They were equal, but with different positions and responsibilities. A perfect team, ruling together on one accord, working side by side in the garden. They had dominion over all things on the earth. This was their assignment from God.

While reading this scripture again, I saw two things I had never seen before about the conversation between Eve and the Serpent. The first mistake Eve made was that she listened to the serpent. When he realized she was listening to him, he continued, for he knew then that she was considering what he was saying. And that is what she did; she considered his words over what God said. She allowed her thoughts to take precedence over what God said. When she did this, she became an easy target. Thus, satan was on his way to successfully catching his prey with the bait.

Eve allowed the serpent to convince her to question and doubt God's commandment and character. The serpent questioned Eve on what God said. He knew what God said, but he wanted to know if she knew what He'd said. Satan wanted to see if she believed in her heart what God said was true. He wanted to find out if she knew who she really was. Sadly, we know the answer to this.

The second thing Eve did wrong was to answer the serpent. She had already given thought to his question; however, it would have been just that-- a thought. But she made the fatal mistake of answering him, and this is where the deceit came in. This is where he beguiled her into believing a lie, which ultimately caused her to lose her identity.

Remember, *"The thief comes to steal, kill and destroy...,"* John 10:10. He is not coming with a long pitchfork in a red suit with pointed horns, too ugly and hideous to look upon, as society and movies have portrayed him. He is going to come very subtly, as he did with Eve. He will appear as an angel of light, beautiful and appealing, yet sly and cunning. His job, especially regarding Christians, is to distract and deceive us from the very things of God.

The serpent questioned Eve, who listened and responded to him. It was bad enough that Eve listened to satan, but when she responded to his question, this gave him the opportunity he needed to make Eve not only question what God said, but to act contrary to what God said. He encouraged her to reason with what God said, and that's when doubt came upon her: *"And the serpent said unto the woman, Ye shall not surely die: [5] For God doth know that in the day ye eat thereof, then your eyes shall be opened, and ye shall be as gods, knowing good and evil,"* Genesis 3:1-5.

In that split second, the fall was inevitable. She lost all sense of her identity and knowledge as to why she was created. She began to doubt what God said. Once she entertained his words, satan was able to mess with her mind. From the moment she believed the devil's lie, the enemy was able to deceive Eve into wanting to be something other than who she was. She felt God had shortchanged her and did not have her best interests at heart. Sadly, and unfortunately, she wanted more, without realizing that she already had it all. Everything she was looking for and wanted was already in her. Let me put it more clearly, before the fall, Eve had everything, after the fall, she lost it all.

When God saw what she had done, He said, *"I will greatly mul tiply thy sorrow and thy conception; in sorrow thou shalt bring forth children; and thy desire shall be to thy husband, and he shall rule over thee,"* Genesis 3:16. An interesting observation is that prior to the fall, the Lord never had to speak these words to Eve because there was no need. Up until that time, she walked in her identity. I can only imagine what it was like to walk in the garden in the cool of the day when the Lord came down to fellowship with both Adam and Eve. Their conversation had nothing to do with an identity issue. However, after the fall, things drastically changed on earth. Sin came into the world and order was lost. The battle of position between man and woman ensued. One was ordained to lead, while the other was ordained to follow.

Satan deceived the woman, convincing her to be something other than what she was created to be. Initially, I believe Eve thought she was helping her husband, but the more she listened to satan, the more she began to see things differently. Maybe she thought she should have been the one in charge, and her husband her help meet. Or maybe she perceived that she knew better than God, or that God was keeping everything to Himself. No one really knows what went through her mind, but it does appear that she wanted to be just like God. She wanted to be the man, because subconsciously, by eating the forbidden fruit, her actions were displaying she didn't want the man or God to lead her. Defying God's authority, she was deciding what was best for her. Because of this, from that time on, the Lord has bestowed rules and guidelines on the woman. He had to restore order in the Kingdom, giving the man and the woman specific assignments to maintain order.

The Lord told Eve that her desire was to be for her husband and that he was to have rule over her. This was how it was in the beginning, but it didn't have to be stated—it was just so. Adam and Eve side by side. Adam was the head because there had to be someone in authority for order to be established. In return, Adam covered Eve with love, protection, warmth, and security. The Lord didn't make Eve to be a slave to Adam, but rather a help meet to Adam.

Let me say this just in case you don't already know, the Lord didn't create us to be slaves to our husbands, or to men. He loves His daughters very much. We are very precious in His eyes. Scripture says that we are the "Apple of His Eye". When the Lord created us, it was good. Man needed a help meet, an equal. He did not need another authority figure, for God was his head. He needed someone to reign with him, to assist in ruling the earth with him and to share his identity, but not to become him.

God loves us equally, for He is not a respecter of persons. He is not telling us that women cannot be leaders, nor is he saying that He wants us to be in the home barefoot and pregnant. However, we as women must be mindful that we have some God-ordained responsibilities, as do the men. The Lord wants and needs us to be leaders in the Kingdom. In the Garden of Eden, Adam and Eve ruled together. Eve had to be a leader to even be put in such a position, but she wasn't the head. If you are still having trouble with this concept, look at it this way, someone has to be the head of any organization. Without a leader, there is no order, only chaos and confusion. It is not an ego thing, it's a God thing. Only one person can lead, while the others must follow, while helping him become successful. Even in corporate America, there is only one Chief Executive Officer (CEO).

Before satan came into the picture, I'll bet Eve didn't have a problem being a help meet or submitting to the authority of her husband. It was a way of life for her, and may I add—a very good way of life. As the saying goes in todays' language, she was "living large". In old romance novels the heroine always lived in luxury and privilege. She dined on strawberries, cream and chocolate. Well, if such was Eve's life, she blew it big time.

Now, maybe you're thinking, or saying, *"It wasn't all Eve's fault. Adam had a role in the matter too."* Or perhaps you're thinking, *"It wasn't my fault what Eve did, so why do I have to pay the price for what she did."* I used to feel this way too (maybe not in words, but definitely in my actions). I used to say, *"I'm not going to listen to this garbage. It's my thing. I will do it the way I want to because no one has rule over me."* Well, I did it the way I wanted; and, like Eve; I was deceived and made the wrong choices. As a result, it cost me in many areas.

By being deceived by satan, Eve disrupted the order, forcing God to reestablish it. When we make the wrong choices we disrupt the order, and only God can reestablish it. But thank God there was a plan! God's plan for restoring order after the fall and for our lives was made manifest in the redemptive plan of Jesus Christ, our Lord and Savior. This was, and still is, the only way to get us back to our true identity in Him. As Christian women, our identity first begins with Jesus and in Jesus. It was established in the beginning when God created us. Don't make the same error as Eve, for like Eve, it will cost you.

Section 2. Examples (Spirits) of a Hindering Wife

When the Lord started pressing me to write this book, there were a lot of changes going on in my life-- changes that I didn't welcome. During the process of the changes, the Lord showed me who I really was, versus who I thought I was. For the first time in my life, I saw a person I never knew existed. I didn't have to look at anyone else; all I had to do was look at the reflection in the mirror. Who was this person staring back at me? What was she really like? What did she really want? It's funny how we think we have it all together when we have no clue. This was me. At the age of forty-three, I was still lost.

During this period of examination, I can recall one particular incident that I literally saw how I used to look in the Lord's perspective as far as being a hindrance to my husband. One night while watching a sitcom on television, I saw a woman that reminded me of myself. The only difference was the actress was playing a part; whereas, I was not. The woman and her fiancée were planning to marry soon; however, the relationship was doomed from the start. Because the woman wanted to take the lead in the relationship they argued a lot. One day they were arguing in front of their friends. In the middle of their argument, her fiancé' took off his pants and gave them to her saying, "It's obvious you want to wear them." And it was obvious to everyone except her. She didn't have a clue that her relationship was on the verge of breaking up. Her need to be controlling, bossy, and always right, had led her down this path. She even had the audacity to tell her fiancé in front of everyone that if he wanted to be the head, he should bring in the "head kind of money." You guessed it. She made more money than he did. And she wasn't too humble to let him and others know this.

As women, we tend to applaud this type of behavior, or respond with remarks such as, "You go girl," or "You got it going on." But does she? Or is it just an illusion? Perhaps we're fooling ourselves by thinking that because we have attained status of one kind or an other we have the right to demand control. Needless to say, that girl (like so many of us) went home alone that night.

After watching the program for about fifteen minutes, I turned it off. (I couldn't watch it any more). I kept thinking, "Oh my gosh! That was me! That's exactly how I used to act and what I used to say." With this revelation, I said aloud, "Lord, this is what this book is all about, being a help meet or a hindrance. And in case you haven't figured it out yet, the woman on the television show was definitely a hindrance.

Being a help meet is wonderful. I didn't say easy. I said wonderful. However, being a hindrance is not only a never-ending task, but it is also terribly exhausting. Why? The answer is simple. You can never let your guard down. You're never relaxed. You always have to prove you're in control because you're afraid to be seen as weak, sensitive, or even worse, vulnerable. You always have to prove that you're right, because in your mind you truly believe you are right—at least the majority of the time. This takes a great deal of work. Maybe that's the reason why I was so stressed. It would've been a lot easier on me if I had only given Pete the reigns and let him do it.

As I said earlier, I thought that I was a good help meet to my husband. And for the most part, I was – on the surface that is. I wish I could make you understand how detrimental a hindering wife is to her husband. I wish you could see into my heart, and know what the Lord is revealing to me. I know it makes you feel good to say that you have arrived, or that you've accomplished so much, but if you are honest with yourself, you'll see how empty your life is when you aren't in the proper God-ordained order. When we take on these roles or positions that are not ordained by God (even though the path seems right), in the end they only lead to confusion, pain, and yes, sometimes destruction. We don't have to take the lead in our homes to be important. We don't have to prove that we can do things better than men to be important. We are already important. We are beautifully and wonderfully created by our Heavenly Father. Do you know that it takes a powerful, real, strong woman of God with great faith to submit.

I would like to address some poignant areas to you in regards to being a hindrance to your husband. Allow the Holy Spirit to minister to you, especially if you see yourself in any these…I did.

Now let's read of some examples (spirits) of a hindering wife:

a. I Want To Be the Man

Inadvertently, this is what I was saying to Pete. No, not with words, but definitely with my actions. Many times Pete would tell me, "Fannie I can't be the man because you want the position." He was right, I just didn't know it. Although I was saved, it all boiled down to something I was taught early in my childhood years. What was it? *Self-preservation is the first law of nature.* Meaning: It's all about me, or every man for himself. Even as a young child, my concept of life was, "I am never ever going to allow anyone to stop me from being what I want to be or doing what I want to do. I'm in charge of my own destiny." Notice, I didn't say what the Lord wanted me to be or do. I said what I wanted to be or do. There is a difference.

I've told you about my past and my vow to not let anyone else rule over me. My divorce didn't help the matter. If truth be told, it only made me keep up my guards. When Pete and I got married, the first three years were smooth. But when we moved to a new place, things went from smooth to downright rough. In the past, I was used to making my own decisions. I was doing what I wanted to do, when I wanted, and how I wanted. I was the man, or should I say, I was my own person.

I don't recall struggling for that position in the first three years of our marriage. I don't know if Pete was walking on eggshells just to let me have my way or to keep the peace. We never discussed it. Call it the honeymoon years, I don't know. But, subconsciously, my mind was made up. I wasn't going to change for anyone; and, though I loved Pete, I was not going to change for him either. I was still going to be in charge of my life. Little did I know, I was hindering the marriage from reaching its full potential.

I wanted to be in control (like many women do), because it gives us a semblance of security. I always tell Pete, once you give a woman power; it's hard to take it back. I had no idea that I had to have power, or that I wanted to be in control, until I was put in a situation that threatened my position.

I already informed you that I am classified as a "positive Type A" personality, and for the most part, I agree with the analysis. Although I am, no longer a perfectionist, I still want things done in a spirit of excellence. In the past, I had a terrible time delegating authority. I knew if I did something, it was not only going to be done correctly, but it would also be carried out in an exemplary manner. Unbeknownst to me, being an officer in the military only reinforced the tendency for control. In fact, I had many soldiers (men and women) under my authority. For the most part we had a great love and respect for each other. We were a team, and I was their team leader. But that wasn't the issue. The issue was that once home, I couldn't and didn't separate my professional job from my domestic responsibilities.

For years we would go on and on, fighting a silent war on who was the man; I always had the answers. I always knew what to do or what to say. Many times, I overrode what Pete did or said. Not in his face. I did it behind his back. Now you must know that I didn't for one minute think that I was disrespecting him. I really thought I was helping him. In my twisted thinking, I was quietly saying, "He doesn't know, so since he doesn't and I do, I will help him. After all, I am the help meet." But I was not helping. I hindered him, which made him weak in certain areas. He said that he would rather have peace than to argue, so he backed down and let me have my way. His comment to me was, "You are going to do what you want to do anyway." I didn't even realize that in my quest for wanting to be the man, I was hurting the man, my husband.

It is easy for women, if the man allows it, to take control. I like to say it is in our nature. It's what we learned from the world. So often in the marriage, the wife becomes the central figure in the relationship. She makes the majority of the decisions, including where to go on vacation, what to eat, and what to buy. If she is not careful, she will take on the dominant role, leaving her husband to take second place to her leadership. The minute she begins to assume that she is the head; she becomes a hindrance to her husband.

Women who always have to be right, or want everything their way have a major control issue. It's not okay in any relationship, but it's extremely detrimental in a marriage relationship. If this is a problem for you, search out the root of your need to control. For me, it finally came down to insecurity and past issues. I had never allowed the Lord to totally heal me from the divorce, or from my father's abandonment. I had to prove to Pete, and every other male, that I was competent and they couldn't hurt me. Unfortunately, I took that stronghold with me into my marriage. Even though I was married, I had erected steel walls that even Pete couldn't penetrate. No one was going to hurt me again. I was in charge. I was the man.

When I finally came to myself (which took many years of tears and pain), I grasped the truth. And the truth was that I was not in control, God was. Even now, I am still remorseful for how much I may have hindered Pete's walk. I wonder where we would be if we understood these principles at the outset. I say we'd because Pete had a role in this too. Instead of taking back control, he let me have it. So we both had to change.

Listen to me women of God. Whether you are married, single, or about to get married, you do not have control. You are not the one in charge. Whatever your issue is, get to the root of it before you destroy your relationships. Ask the Holy Spirit to reveal the root cause of your need for control. Is it fear? Is it insecurity and abandonment, like mine was? Is it because you were a spoiled little girl, who still needs to grow up? Is it because you have a problem with authority, or men? Whatever the stronghold is, deal with it and understand that it comes from satan and not from the Lord. The word of God says in Ephesians 6:12, *"For we wrestle not against flesh and blood, but against principalities, against powers, against the rulers of the darkness of this world, against spiritual wickedness in high places."*

If you need help, pray that the Lord will send mature saints to minister to you. A bossy woman may be pleasing to the world, but she is not pleasing to the Lord, or to her husband.

b. I'm Not Your Mother, I'm Your Wife

Believe me when I say that the Holy Spirit birthed this book into my spirit, because originally this section's title was going to be the book's title. Why? Because this is how I felt. It was only after intense deliverance, healing and restoration that I realized the issue went much deeper. Yet it still stands that I am not my husband's mother, I am his wife. Sadly, it was a long time before I could differentiate between the two.

Women are born with nurturing spirits. It is part of our emotional makeup. Most of us want to care for others, whether it's a sick child, a parent, or a friend who's in need. We are caregivers at heart who want others to feel better. It is in us to make others feel good. Before we get the iodine and Band-Aid for a child with a scrape, most likely we'll kiss it to make it feel better. This is what we do for our children, and for some of us, this is what we do for our husbands. We tend to take those nurturing qualities and apply them in our marriages; thus, treating our men more like our children than our husbands. Instead of being his wife, we take on the role of his mother. I know in some instances I did. And yes, it hindered him.

As a child, I watched as my mother modeled the way a mother should act. My parents separated when I was ten years old, and from that time to this day my mother lived for her children. Thrust into being a single parent with five children, her life revolved around us and our lives revolved around her. She was a very good mother. And in spite of the hardship of raising five kids in inner-city Baltimore in the seventies and early eighties, we had a good childhood. I never once saw her become unraveled when the bill collectors came to collect their money. (Back then they came to your door. Today, they just turn off everything via computer from the office.) I'm not sure how she did it, but she took care of everything. We were poor, yet we didn't know it. We always had food on our table and clothes on our backs. So naturally, when I got married, I took on the same role I had learned from my mother. Some positives, some negatives, but this was all I knew.

It was easy. After all, I was dealing with some serious strongholds, so being my husband's caretaker was just part of my perceived role. While he was a good provider, I tended to treat him like my son rather than my husband. Wanting to control as much as I wished to protect him, I took over paying the bills (or rather, I hounded him into letting me pay the bills). I never told him about any bad news, especially when the bill collectors started threatening to turn off our utilities. I never told him how we almost had the home in Texas go into foreclosure, due to not having the money to pay the mortgage. I never informed him of how much we were behind on the bills, or how much we had in the accounts, and so on. Yes, it was his responsibility, and he should have taken a role in our finances; but, every time he questioned or threatened to take over, I told him that everything was fine. By doing this, I crippled him, like many mothers do to their own sons.

By doing everything for Pete, I was hindering him from being my husband and the man God created him to be. I never allowed him to help me with the household chores, the laundry, the cooking, you name it. I told him, "I will take care of it, you go sit down." Even when I was exhausted from a hard day at work, I took care of everything. I was superwoman, or super mom. Was I being a good wife? To a degree I still think I was; however, in all of my good, I was still crippling him.

What do children do when they know mommy is going to take care of everything? They go about their business and do what ever they want to do. They become stifled, stagnated and spoiled, expecting to be waited on rather than learning how to be servants. Why? Because they know their mother will do everything for them. They don't have to make up the bed. They don't have to pick up after themselves. Or in my brother's case, mow the lawn. They know they don't have to do anything because their mommy will do it for them. They don't have to be responsible. As a result, they grow up expecting everything to be provided for or handed to them, with no effort on their part. In the end it does them and society a terrible disservice.

One day as I was talking on the phone to one of my spiritual mentors, my emotions were raw, mentally and spiritually overwhelmed, I was venting to her about Pete. I felt as if Pete didn't care. She listened as I vented. After I got everything off of my chest, she began to speak. She told me that she felt led by the Holy Spirit to tell me that the problem wasn't Pete per se, it was me-- I was an enabler. (That was the first time I'd ever heard the word). She continued to comment on how Pete didn't have to do anything, because I did everything for him. Why should he pick up after himself, help with the housework, cook or clean, if I was doing it all for him. She basically told me that if I was to be angry at someone, the finger should be pointed at me, not Pete, because in a sense, I was making him useless. Ouch! Her words really hurt, but I knew that she was telling the truth. I was Pete's enabler. I was trying to be his mother, by kissing the scrapes so they didn't hurt. I kept him from making decisions for us, whether wrong or right. In my mind, I seriously thought that I was protecting him by keeping bad news from him. But in actuality, I had both disabled and hindered him.

It is the Holy Spirit's job to enable us to go the right way, to seek guidance from the Lord, and to empower us. Without realizing it, I was trying to be those things for Pete. But I am not the Holy Spirit; and by taking His place, I was out of order. I nearly destroyed myself and the marriage in the process.

I missed so many opportunities to be with my husband when he would ask if I needed help around the house; especially when we were getting ready for company. Many times he would ask, but I would tell him that I had everything under control and to just relax. I missed opportunities for Pete to take over and fix problems because I didn't tell him how bad the finances were, or our situation was. If only I would have said, "Pete, I need your help," or "Pete, I can't fix this, can you?" But I didn't. It would have made me appear to be weak, like I didn't have it all together. Talk about stress. During those five years my doctors visits increased by fifty percent.

Being a wife doesn't mean that you are the one to carry the load all by yourself. You can't and you are not supposed to because you are not equipped. You and your husband are a team. Allow him to assist you in the household work and in your children's activities. Don't try to protect him from bad news. Tell him, and then allow him as the head to make the decision pertaining to the news. He is your husband, not your child. Believe me, he is equipped to handle the role. Don't hinder him from the chance to emerge as the leader he was born to be. Again, God designed couples to work as a team because together they can achieve more.

c. He Is Not Your Daddy

I have asked quite a number of single women their reasons for wanting to get married, and do you know what the overwhelming majority say, "I want a husband so he can take care of me." Sadly, many women want to get married so they can be taken care of by a man. I have news for these women. If this is your only reason for getting married then you are living in a fantasy world. You are in a dream, and you need to wake up. If you want to get married just so that a man will take care of you, you are not ready for marriage. Instead of a husband, you want a "Sugar Daddy". Marriage is about two people taking care of each other. Don't get me wrong. As married women we do want our husbands to provide for us; after all, he is the head. However, as help meets we are also responsible to help him in whatever ways we can.

When I hear women call their husbands or boyfriends "Daddy" or "Sugar Daddy" I cringe. Don't shoot me down. Let's keep it all in perspective. I am not referring to how my sister would sometimes call her husband "daddy" in front of the kids in order for them to understand specific roles in the house. Nor am I referring to you calling your husband "daddy" in a playful intimate way. I am speaking about women who use those terms because they want a "daddy" instead of a husband.

When people would jokingly ask if Pete was my "Daddy" I would respond, "No, he is my husband. I don't and can't do the things I do with and to Pete to my father." Graphic, I know. But that is the truth. Pete is not my daddy. He is my husband, and I am his wife.

I am going to be blunt here and say that a woman who just wants a man to take care of her, while she does nothing at all (not even cook, clean, or work), is just plain old lazy and a hindrance to her mate. She has taken the concept of "provider" to a level that God never intended. The position of help meet was designed to be a blessing. And whether you believe it or not, a man may put up with a dirty, unorganized home because he loves you; however, this is not what he wants.

As a little girl, your father (or other authoritative figures in your life; mine was my grandfather), treated you like the young girl you were. At times, he would buy you nice clothes, or some Barbie doll or toy you just had to have. You probably had him wrapped around your finger. Spoiled, you got everything your heart desired. That was as a little girl. That was your father or someone you looked up to like a father figure.

Now that you are married, you cannot expect your husband to take on the same role. Don't treat him as though he is your daddy. Don't expect him to take care of all your needs. Don't expect him to do all of the work, cook, clean, and take care of the kids, while you shop or look at television all day. I know I am in somebody's house! Don't even expect him to take care of all of the finances. Learn to budget a checking account. One of the saddest things I encountered during the first Gulf War was the alarming number of the wives who husbands were fighting the war that were left behind had no idea how to manage their finances. Not even how to balance a check book. What unnecessary pressure on the husband, because while he was trying to fight a war, his mind was also wondering who was going to take care of his wife while he was away! Do you think his mind was 100% on the war?

I have some special young female friends: Adrian, Avis and Neasell, who have incredible relationships with their fathers. They were definitely their daddies' little girls, and forever they will be. They are married now, and although they love and respect their fathers, they have become wives. Watching them a couple of years ago, I have noticed how much they have grown up to be beautiful women of God, and now beautiful wives to their husbands. They have stepped out of one role and into another, just as God intended. They know that their husbands are not their daddies.

d. The Know It All Wife

No question about it- this best described me. Of course at the time, I never would have admitted this; particularly when my husband would tell me in the not-so-pleasant tone, "You think you know everything. You're never wrong." Does this sound familiar? Are you a know-it-all wife too?

There is a difference between a know-it-all wife and a nagging wife; yet, both are extremely detrimental to the marriage relationship. I am ashamed to admit this, but my background, degree and professional status, inspired the illusion that I was a woman of great stature. I perceived that I was successful as far as the world was concerned, and sadly, my success went to my head. I didn't know that it did until the Lord called me out of the military. It was then that I felt I had to prove my value, not only to the world but also to my husband. You might think that I'm being a little hard on myself. Maybe I am, but I want to make you understand, that this is where I was, so you don't have to go there. I have to be honest so that if you need deliverance in this area, you can be set free.

There is nothing worse than a woman who thinks she knows everything. Not only is she a hindrance to her husband, but she can become obnoxious to everyone she encounters. Before I understood God's take on this issue, I would often correct my husband, telling him outright that he was wrong. I always offered my opinion on every subject whether he asked for it or not. I always had a solution and a better way to do things, and I made sure that he knew it, because I had to have the last word. Unfortunately, this went on for years. It's not that I didn't trust his judgment; it's just that I trusted my judgment more. Oh, don't let him go against my opinion, especially if I really knew I was right. I would often call others to tell them what Pete was doing wrong, and because of our relationship they would often support my position. Pete called them my cheer leading squad. I had to be right. My pride and ego simply wouldn't allow me to be wrong.

Help Meet Or Hindrance: Which One Are You?

As much as I hate to admit it, I would also undermine the way he did things by going behind him, checking, fixing, and even changing things if I thought it was necessary. Whenever we had a Bible study, after he gave the lesson (you guessed it), I would add my two cents. This led to many heated arguments, after which he would withdraw, which only made me angrier. My response to his withdrawal was, "You think I don't know anything." It got so bad that we just stopped doing Bible study.

This was more than me merely wanting to be the boss or the man (although the two issues are related). This was about the Lord dealing with my pride issue. I felt that He had stripped me from the very thing I needed to survive, so I had to prove to myself and everyone else that I was right. I was significant. And although many times I was right, the problem wasn't me being right per se, the problem was I had to be right at all costs. I was adamant and unyielding, much like a lawyer proving his case before the jury.

It got so bad that Pete refused to tell me his plans, specifically with what the Lord was telling him to do. Because believe it or not, I actually thought that the Lord spoke to Pete through me. Talk about being deceived. We as women must be careful. Why? Because as wives, we do have discerning spirits, which some call a sixth sense, but it's actually the Holy Spirit within us. It is true that the Lord does speak to us concerning our husbands and children. But as far as our husbands are concerned, when God speaks to us regarding some areas in their lives that may be out of sync, He may only want us to pray, rather than confront him about the area. I had to learn this lesson the hard way, and frankly, I am still learning.

While there were times when I was correct, there were other times when I was dead wrong, and in the long run it cost us. It finally got to the point that Pete wouldn't tell me anything. When I would question him about this, he would say, "You think you know everything" or "Why bother, you never listen." I didn't realize what I was doing was making him feel incompetent. It would upset me to no end when he would consult others for information I would have gladly given him. When I asked him about it, again he would say, "You never listen to me" or "I don't like talking to you about these matters because you think you're always right." As you can imagine those comments made me even more furious and insecure, to the point whereas, I wanted more control just to prove I was right and he was wrong. I didn't realize this until years later, after I'd been delivered from my control issues. One day we were talking and I apologized for always thinking that I was right. I asked him if he had known that I struggled in this area. He said yes, but due to my struggles, he had to step back, be quiet, and let the Lord handle the matter.

If you have problems in this area, ask yourself (please be honest), "Why do I feel the need to be right all of the time?" Mine was a deep-rooted pride issue. I wasn't aware of it until I grew weary of always carrying such a heavy load. Women who have to be right all the time strip their husbands of their manhood and can actually be operating in the spirit of witchcraft. The truth is no one but the Lord is right all of the time. Even if you are right, know when to fight your instinct to tell your husband you have a better way. Ask the Holy Spirit to help you. Make sure your way isn't condescending and doesn't belittle your husband. Share it in the spirit of love and humility, so he can receive it and maintain his dignity. No one likes a person who thinks they are right all the time. As hard as it is to swallow, you may be a bossy controlling woman who needs to be delivered from such strongholds.

Many times, even when I was right, I still lost the battle because it only pushed my husband away. It wasn't until years later he was finally able to trust me with his plans. Now I listen more, and speak less. If he is wrong, I still fight the urge to tell him so, and I don't speak about doing it my way. Though at times it's not easy, I depend on the Holy Spirit to guide my husband to the truth, or to allow me to tell him in a spirit of humbleness and love so that he can receive it. Ladies, isn't that more important than being right?!

In my deliverance of always having to be right, I've come to realize that I don't know everything. And now I tell people I don't know anything unless Jesus tells me. Is this an excuse or a cop out? No. This is my reality. For you see, my pride in this area was leading me down the path of destruction. What was I profiting by being right all of the time? What did I gain? What do you gain? I have learned that when you know who you are in the Lord, you don't have to prove yourself to others or try to appear to be better than you really are. In addition, it takes a wise person to keep quiet and listen. Whether right or wrong, a wise person knows that he doesn't have to prove his point. Always keep in mind; the truth will wear out a lie.

Bite your tongue, chew your lip, hold your breath while counting to ten, or pray without ceasing. Do whatever it takes to refuse to listen to the whisper in your head, and stifle the need to be right and have an answer for everything. Remember, balance is the key. When you see your husband heading down the wrong path, or doing something questionable, immediately start praying for the Lord to intervene; or, ask Him if you should speak to your husband about the matter. But wait on the Lord for direction. And please, if you do speak, make sure that your words are kind, loving, and seasoned with salt. Your words will either tear down or build up- so great power is in the tongue.

Also, when your husband speaks, whether it is significant or insignificant to you, give him the courtesy of listening to him. Do not butt in—just listen. Many times he doesn't need a response; he just wants you to listen. In the end, he'll work things out. As I mentioned earlier, this was a huge problem in my life. I often interrupted when my husband was speaking—to put in my two cents. This really frustrated him, especially when it happened in a group setting. But because he hated public confrontation, he would step aside and allow me to speak.

For you see, my problem was that I felt I had to prove I was just as knowledgeable as he was and basically that's all any know-it all-wife is doing. She is competing with her husband, trying to prove that she's either equal or superior. There's no doubt, this type of behavior is destructive to the relationship, and it only shows her insecurities.

e. The Nagging Wife

One detrimental way a wife can be a hindrance to her husband is to nag and complain all the time. In fact, if you ask many men, this is one of the major problems in the marriage; their wife nags or complains all the time. It's so bad for some of them that they don't like going home. They can put up with everything else but the nagging. To be honest, no one likes to be around a nagging, complaining woman. I have a good friend and every time I call her she has something to complain about. After speaking with her, I would feel so down that I eventually stopped calling her as much. Can you imagine how a husband feels if he has to deal with this all day long, seven days a week? Fortunately, that's one problem I did not have. Thank God, because with all of the other issues I had, I don't think my poor husband could have dealt with that one too. I don't think we would have made it.

To inform you how bad it is to be a nagging wife, the Bible has quite a few scriptures on the subject:

Proverbs 19:13 (NLT)
 "A foolish child is a calamity to a father; *a nagging wife annoys like a constant dripping.*"

Proverbs 14:1 (NLT)
 "A wise woman builds her house; *a foolish woman tears hers down with her own hands.*"

Proverbs 9:13 (NLT)
 "*The woman named Folly is loud and brash. She is ignorant and doesn't even know it.*"

Proverbs 21:9 (NLT)
 "*It is better to live alone in the corner of an attic than with a contentious wife in a lovely home.*"

Proverbs 21:19 (NLT)
"*It is better to live alone in the desert than with a crabby, complaining wife.*"

Proverbs 12:4 (NLT)
"A worthy wife is her husband's joy and crown; *a shameful wife saps his strength.*"

Proverbs 27:15-16 (NLT)
"*A nagging wife is as annoying as the constant dripping on a rainy day. [16] Trying to stop her complaints is like trying to stop the wind or hold something with greased hands.*"

The word *contentious* is defined as strife; an idea or point *in which a person argues*. The word *strife* is defined as conflict, fight, struggle, discord, etc. For further reading on the subject, I highly recommend Joyce Meyer's book, "*Life Without Strife.*" It really helped me to understand this issue, and it may help you too.

When I got married, I realized that all men, including my husband, have egos. Its part of their make-up and it's real. However, how they deal with their ego is up to the individual. Many times, for women in today's culture, it is difficult to acknowledge that our counterparts have egos and that they need to protect them. Why? Quite simple. We don't have time to deal with or stroke anyone's ego but our own. Without getting into a heated discussion, my point is that no man (or in this case husband), likes to hear that he is inadequate, or not living up to his role as a caregiver and provider; especially if he is doing his best. Pete used to say that a man doesn't need a wife telling him what he is not doing. He needs a wife to encourage him, not tear him down. Ouch! I am afraid that this is what many of us are doing. We are tearing down our men, our marriages, and in the process we are destroying our homes.

I know men are not perfect, and yours in particular may not be. But, if this is why you feel the need to nag, I urge you to seek wise spiritual council while praying and fasting for your husband. Again, to be clear, I am referring to women whose husbands are trying and doing the best they can, and yet they still nag. Maybe you do this because your mother nagged your father, maybe it's a generational iniquity. Whatever it is, it's destroying your marriage.

Look at the Book of Proverbs as it pertains to a nagging, contentious wife: She tears her house down; she's foolish; she saps her husband's strength; she's ignorant and doesn't know it; her husband would rather live in an attic or in the desert than with her; she's annoying; and a constant drip that cannot be stopped. I'll bet you never realized how you looked to your husband and to God when you're nagging. (Arguing here and there is one thing, but consistently nagging is another).

Now look what it says about a woman who doesn't nag her husband: A worthy wife is her husband's joy and crown; a wise woman builds her house; the peace and stability of her home are the result of her choice to be encouraging and helpful. A wise wife realizes that her husband is not perfect, yet she supports him in his imperfections; she provides sweet, kind words, to make him feel he is capable; for he knows she loves him regardless, and for that he loves her with all his manly might; a wise woman gently pushes her husband into the path he must go; she helps him; she makes him feel blessed, a king in his own home; and he in turn, is her covering under the authority of God. What a difference!

The foolish wife, with her constant nagging, breaks her husband down. His constant need or attempt to please her brings other calamities upon his life, such as health issues, oppression, depression, and in the end, it could lead to a spiritual meltdown. He has no time to worry about pleasing the Lord, because he is always trying to placate his wife. His need for peace, security and purpose, may unfortunately lead him to infidelity, substance abuse, pornography, or even to be a workaholic. In addition, the constant nagging and negativity leaves him insecure, and makes him question his competence as a man. Her words destroy the very foundation of his manhood, breaking down his ego and thwarting his purpose in God.

(Just a note, in regards to adultery or other sins that may derive from a wife nagging; regardless of how bad the situation is, this still does not give the man or anyone the reason or excuse to sin. No one is to blame for someone sinning. That is a choice that individual makes. We all have the choice of right or wrong; so, if someone says you are the cause of the sin, that is not true—you may have had a part, but that person made the decision to sin).

I have found that women who constantly nag or complain normally have other deep rooted issues. Most likely, because the nagging wife doesn't feel good about herself, her inner fears and doubts cause her to lash out on those closest to her, specifically her husband. Because she is unfulfilled, she expects her husband to fill the void, but he cannot. The job is too big for him to fulfill on his own, which makes her more demanding. If truth be told, in her subconscious mind, she knows it's not him, it's really her.

Ask yourself, "Do I constantly feel the need to nag or complain about my husband?" Then ask, "Is it helping or hindering my marriage?" Then take a good look in the mirror and ask yourself, "Does the problem stem from him, or is it really me?" If it is him, pray. But if it is determined that it is you, find out the root behind the spirit by asking the Holy Spirit, and continue to pray to the Lord for healing and deliverance. Prayer really does change things.

I leave you with this: A wife has the power build her home, or tear down her house.

f. The Spoiled (Controlling) Little Girl

As a child, I remember there was always one little girl in the group who wanted her way, and if we didn't give in, she wouldn't let us play with her toys. If she couldn't get her way, she pouted, until finally, to keep peace, everyone gave in to pacify her. We used to call her a spoiled brat, but in actuality she was manipulating and controlling. I guarantee that she knew what she was doing to get her way. All she had to do was make others feel sorry for her by posing as the victim. As she grew up, she was considered popular. She was the one who dictated what the crowd did, wore, and even talked about. (Of course not all popular people are like this, this is just an example.) Perhaps she is this way because her parents gave her everything and she never went without. As a result she feels that the world and others owe her the same treatment. Perhaps she deals with a deep-rooted strong hold, an insecurity issue, or an identity crisis. She doesn't know who she really is, so to keep her secret from being revealed, she uses control and manipulation in her relationships; whining, pouting and crying are her weapons of mass destruction.

Now suppose this girl grows into adulthood without ever being delivered from her need to be the *queen*. She gets married and brings those demons from her past into her marriage. Sadly, she doesn't even know that they're there. She still feels she has every right to get whatever she wants. After all, the world revolves around her. Doesn't it? She is the victim. Do you see where I am going here?

It's okay for a husband to want the best for his wife. Indeed, he should want the best for her. And as wives, we should be spoiled by our husbands to a degree. However, for our purpose here, we are talking about someone who uses manipulation and control to get what she wants. Once married, you must come to terms with the truth. And the truth is… your days of being a spoiled, pampered little girl are over. Your husband didn't marry a princess, he married a wife. Therefore, you are no longer daddy's little girl, you are someone's wife.

Let me carefully explain the point I am trying to get across to you. The wife's role is extremely important to the success of her husband. (I know we have established this, but please listen with your spiritual ears, or read with your spiritual eyes). If the wife is not careful, she could easily cause her husband to stumble and possibly fall if her mannerism is that of a child instead of his wife. Because of her spoiled ways, she can easily manipulate her husband into thinking he is following the Lord, when in actuality, he's not. He is following her leading. All the while, she is deceiving herself into thinking that she is helping him.

Unfortunately, I must confess that on very few occasions, I have done this to my husband. I admit I have used manipulation to get my way. (I am serious when I say very few times. I don't like to play in this arena. I know how detrimental this can be). With sincere remorse each time, I did repent of my actions to both my husband and the Lord. One thing I really love about my husband is that he very rarely succumbs to me when I am operating in the spirit of manipulation. He always tells me that he is going to follow God and not me. However, on those rare occasions when he does give in, we usually pay. Perhaps not then, but eventually we do.

If you whine, pout, or use the silent treatment to manipulate your husband into getting your way be careful. There is strong possibility you are walking in witchcraft. By the way, using sex (whether you withhold it, or use it to get your way) as a manipulation tool is very wrong.

Because he loves you, your husband wants to please you and be your knight in shining armor. And to keep peace, he will weaken at your request (or in this case manipulation), and succumb to your plea. What you fail to comprehend is that in your feeble, manipulating and controlling attempt, yes, you are definitely getting your way, winning your victory, but at what cost? What price did you have to pay? Spirits operating under control or manipulation always lose. And spiritually, not only do you lose, but your husband loses also. Your manipulation has stripped him of his manhood. He now depends on you rather than on the Lord. He seeks you before he seeks the Lord. He values your opinion more than he values the Word of God. You both may not see this, but others do, and more importantly, God does.

I've told you that in the process of me dying to self, Pete became mean, and turned into Mr. Hyde. But what you may not understand is that he wasn't really mean at all. He was however, finally taking his rightful place in our marriage as the head of our home. No longer could I use control, manipulation, pouts and whines to get my way. He was becoming forceful, strong, competent, and the man God intended for him to be as my husband. At first, his sternness and forcefulness took me by surprise, especially when he said no and stuck to his guns. But, I must admit, I love him now even more. I rarely (God is still working on me) question him regarding ministry and the running of the house. When the flesh tries to rise up for control, and my feelings get hurt, I know it's the Lord still working on me in this area. He is telling me I need to grow up. Believe me our marriage is better and we are now walking on one accord.

Let me say this- if you are operating with the spirit of a spoiled, controlling, little girl, you my friend need to grow up. Whatever your stronghold is, ask the Lord to reveal it to you, and believe me He will. If necessary, seek wisdom from other mature women of God regarding this area. You have delayed your husband's destiny long enough with your pouting and whining. While being spoiled may be cute for a child, it's ugly in a woman.

Another thing, now that you are married, you may still be "daddy's little girl" to your father, but you have a husband now. Therefore, you can't always run to your daddy when things don't go your way, or when you want something that is not in the budget. Allow your husband to be the man of the house and not your father. Remember, you wanted a husband. If you wanted to continue to be "daddy's spoiled little girl", you should have stayed single.

g. Worldly Hindrances

This is probably one of the most difficult topics to address, and most likely where I will get the least amens. However, I strongly know this has to be discussed, so that we as Christian women can put godly things back into perspective.

Earlier we discussed how the enemy beguiled Eve in the Garden of Eden. And just like the enemy beguiled Eve, the enemy is still beguiling us today. No, he is not using a piece of fruit to spark a discussion, but his tactics are still the same. He is still asking, *"What did God say?"* He wants to know if today's women of God know what God says about us. Unfortunately, if we're honest, we are like Eve; we really don't know what God said, and many of us may not want to know, because like Eve, we want to do our own thing.

Today, satan beguiles us to accommodate our perceived modern day sophistication, or should I say what we believe are important to us as women: power, success and independence. Three major areas of his tactics are: (1) The Corporate Woman, (2) The Women's Liberation Movement, and (3) The Women's Empowerment Movement.

As I stated, this is a difficult topic for me to address, so please listen with your spiritual ears and read with your spiritual eyes. Then you will be able to relate to where I am coming from, and hopefully see that these are not only my ideas. Remember, I too thought this way. Before I discuss these three areas, I want to reiterate that there is nothing wrong with a woman having an outside profession. God has ordained many women to be doctors, lawyers, politicians, directors, CEOs, and other great professions for the Kingdom. Look at Deborah in the book of Judges 4:4. The Lord appointed her as a Judge for His people. She had the responsibility of assisting the man of God to victory in battle. All the same, with all her responsibilities, she never forgot her role as woman. So please do not put yourself in bondage. Just take heed to the Holy Spirit as He speaks to you regarding these three areas.

In regards to worldly hindrances, unfortunately, I'm afraid that even in the Christian arena, we as women have swallowed the world's notion of success, rather, than consulting God on the subject. His ways may often seem outdated, one-sided, hard to accomplish, and for the most part, not always pleasing to one's views. In truth, the Lord's way demands great self-sacrifice, and requires us to depend on Him and to take the role of a servant. All of these things go against our natural bend, what we are taught, and shamefully what we believe in.

Before you try to argue your point, ponder on these questions: By following the ways of the world, did it bring total satisfaction, peace and joy? Has it taken you to the place you longed to go? You know the place I am referring to, the place deep in your heart that no one knows about but you and the Lord? Most of us would have to admit, by following the world it has been nothing but over-whelming and unfulfilling, leaving us feeling somewhat empty inside.

Here are some additional questions I would like you to answer or meditate on: How's your spiritual walk? Are you too busy with worldly matters and goals to seek God everyday? Are you too busy to pray for your husband, your children and yourself? How's your home life? Be honest. I am not talking about if your home is neat and orderly. I'm asking you about your relationship with your husband and your children? Are you and your husband portrayed as husband and wife? Or are the two of you just roommates, living under the same roof, but having different lives? How about the kids? Do you know where they are and what they're doing? Do you know their friends and the parents of their friends? Are they dealing in substance abuse, or sexual sins? Teenage pregnancy doesn't only exist in the secular world. The church is also affected.

Another question is how's your health? Did you know that women today have more health issues than they did thirty years ago? According to the American Heart Association, heart disease is the number one killer among women. And let's talk about stress! Today's women are stressed out to the max. Being CEO's, taking care of our bosses, husbands, children, shopping, carpooling are just a few. We go on- non-stop. Taking care of everyone needs, but our own. Now answer these final questions. "Is your career or profession worth the sacrifices of you, your family, your home life, your health and your time? Did money, fame, prestige and power make you happy? Were they worth the sacrifices?

Remember how in the Garden of Eden satan beguiled Eve into thinking that God was holding out on her? In her mind, she felt a sudden sense of dissatisfaction with what she had, causing her to want more. Her need for more, and to be more, cost her her life. It cost her things that were already hers: peace, prosperity, joy, and an intimate relationship with the Father. Well, just like he deceived Eve, satan wants you to believe that you need more to satisfy your quest for success. Don't believe me? Well, do the following phrases mean anything to you, "I'm every woman, " and my favorite, "I can bring home the bacon, stir it up in a pan, and never let you forget you're a man."

I believe one of the reasons God called me out of the military was because He knew the path I was heading down was not best for me. Though I knew the Lord, I was doing my own thing and going my own way. The Lord knew my makeup and personality. If I was still in the military, I don't know where I'd be today. Sure I would have the rank, the money, the power and prestige, but at what cost? Would I be divorced, or have a separate life, living apart from my husband? I know one thing, if I had stayed in the military, I wouldn't be where I am today spiritually. Don't misconstrue what I'm saying. In the beginning, it wasn't easy giving up my career. It was very hard and painful. It took me five years to let it go. I yearned to go back to what I knew, especially when things got hard financially for us. In fact, in the fall of 2000, I did go back.

It was one of the biggest mistakes I'd ever made, and it almost cost me my marriage and possibly my life. Pete and I were not in agreement with me going back into the military. We had a huge argument over this, probably the biggest one we ever had. But me being me, still wanting to be in control went along with my plans anyway. I called a recruiter for the Army Reserves. I had heard that the reserves needed officers, so within a couple of days, I was back in the Army and about to make Major. The feeling didn't last long. By the end of the week, I knew I had made a mistake. I immediately began to pray for a way out. If I had stayed in, I would have been shipped to the Gulf War in January 2001. My reserves unit was headed there, and I was scheduled to go with them.

The Lord gave me favor with my commander, who assisted me in getting out. Now when people inquire if I am happy or miss the military, I tell them the truth. I miss the camaraderie, the structure, and mission, yet I don't miss it. God has better plans for me. If I had stayed in, I would have been a great hindrance to my husband and our marriage. Instead of thinking about ministry, my husband would have been worrying about whether or not his wife was safe in Iraq. I recently heard that one of my peers made Lieutenant Colonial. I'm ecstatic for her. Maybe that is where I would be if I had continued on that path, but the path I now walk is best for me.

Now let's discuss those three areas that beguile women in a worldly perspective:

The Corporate Woman:

As I was writing this book, the Holy Spirit prodded me to look at a particular movie; so, one night Pete and I watched the movie together. (For copyright reasons I won't mentioned the name). At the conclusion of the movie, I understood why the Lord pricked my heart to watch it. Clearly, the woman in the movie was the epitome of corporate success. Although it was fictional, it depicted real life and what we as women have sacrificed to be a part of the corporate world.

In the movie, the CEO was a successful woman of prominence. On the surface, she had everything: money, prestige, fame, and power. She even had the power to ruin others' careers. Whatever she wanted was at her beck and call. Her peers and subordinates respected her, yet feared, and for the most part, despised her. It appeared that she was in control of her destiny, calling her own shots. She was a bossy, manipulative bully. (Not at all the characteristics God wants in a Godly woman or a help meet.) When she hired a new assistant, she manipulated the young woman into changing who she was; eventually, the young woman began to emulate her boss in every facet. As a result, the assistant did change—losing herself, her dreams, and her identity.

Even though the movie was make believe, the lesson was obvious and the lie was still there. Satan deceived two people (the boss and the assistant) into thinking they had to become someone or something else in order to succeed according to the world's standards.

As I watched the movie from a spiritual standpoint, I began to see the many parallels to this book. On the surface, the woman portrayed as the CEO in the movie was indeed the epitome of success and grandeur. Admired, envied, and fascinating, she was the toast of the business world. However, in truth, her life was anything but what it was perceived from the outside looking in. It was a total mess. In her quest for success, she encountered two failed marriages and her children were raised by everyone but her, their mother. She had learned to suppress her emotions so much that she didn't believe she was responsible for her failed marriages or her unruly kids. (What a deception from the enemy!) The tragedy was that she never acknowledged the truth for what it was. She cared so much about what others thought of her, her position and her prestige, that she willingly sacrificed her family for her career. In the end, it looked as if she had won. But in reality, she had really lost and she was lost. Yes, she was perfect image of a successful woman, but at what cost? She had sacrificed her femininity, her husband, her children, and her life. She had traded her very soul for corporate success. When her assistant started getting to see the real woman behind the position, she realized two very vital factors: (1) her boss didn't have it all together, and more importantly (2) she didn't want to be like her boss anymore. (I like to believe that the boss knew she was living a lie, but couldn't verbally admit it.)

You might say that I'm "stretching the truth"; after all, it's Hollywood at its best. However, if you believe the lie like the woman portraying the CEO in the movie, you too are in big trouble. As a woman of God, a wife and/or mother, ask yourself this question, "At what cost should I gain the world, but lose the very things that are most precious to me?" *"For what is a man profited, if he shall gain the whole world, and lose his own soul? or what shall a man give in exchange for his soul?,"* Matthew 16:26 (KJV).

God has ordained women to leadership positions in the corporate arena, but it's vital that we keep our focus on God to maintain balance. The Lord wants us to be a success in whatever He has called us to do. Remember- there is only one way to be successful, and that is to discover your purpose in God and His Kingdom, and function in it accordingly. That is how we as Christian women should measure success.

The Women's Liberation Movement (or The Feminist Movement)

As a child of the sixties and the seventies, I saw a lot of changes in women. Growing up in the eighties and nineties, I supported and participated in these new changes. Yet in all the changes I have seen in women, I can't figure out the changes that are happening to the women in the twenty first century- the millennium women. What is going on with them?

Being a woman is wonderful and I wouldn't trade it for anything. We are unique creatures created by our Heavenly Father. For this reason, I loved looking at photos of women from my grandmother's era because they appeared so feminine and dainty. The women in the pictures portrayed women. They wore white gloves and beautiful dresses, not tight fitting, but decent and modest. From what my grandmother told me, they depicted the essence of a woman. I guess that's why I like watching old black and white movies and television shows. The women in these shows (for the most part) were not portrayed as sex kittens, vixens, or backstabbing manipulated villains. (And the ones that were portrayed like this, often times didn't have a happy ending). In my eyes, they represented me as a woman-- feminine, dainty, proper and pleasant. You know sugar and spice and everything nice. Now, I know that those movies and television shows were not real, but excluding some of the portrayals, I still enjoyed watching these women.

I don't know about the women's liberation movement from an expert point of view. However, I do agree with some who have stated that it didn't help women as much as they thought it would. In truth, it hurt us. Instead of gaining our independence, it took away from us our very identities as women.

Two factors I do recall about the Women's liberation in the sixties and seventies are: The burning of the bra, and the sexual revolution. As far as the burning of the bra era, it didn't last long. Women who stopped wearing bras soon began to sag. They realized they needed bras, because no one wants saggy breast. Why do you think push up and padded bras were invented? And as far as the sexual revolution, I believe we may have gained sexual satisfaction, but at what cost? STD's, HIV, teenage pregnancy, unwed mothers, and same sex relationships are on the rise. So ask yourself, "Did we truly gain anything from this revolution?" Sure we can satisfy our flesh with sexual pleasures, but even with this there is a risk. So is it really freedom or bondage? Did we really gain what we were fighting for?

These days our little girls think it's okay to dress like ladies of the night. You used to be able to tell them apart, but now you can't. And let's talk about music videos. All you hear and see is sex. These videos make sex seem so pleasurable and enjoyable (and it is… if you are married) but, anything done sexually outside of marriage is sin… *that's the Word!* Anyway, back to the videos. It's crazy how you always see the girls half naked in weird sexual positions, gyrating their bodies all over the place, but you never see the males half-naked? Exploitation at its finest, and yet we truly believe we are free. We believe it is okay.

It seems to me that the whole women's liberation movement was about women wanting to be equal to men. We were. Now we are not. Not the way we think anyway. I said it before, when a wife wants to take on her husband's role in the marriage; she is basically saying she doesn't know who she is in Jesus Christ. When she feels the need to compete with him in everything- money, position, and authority—believing she can do better than him, there are some serious problems in the marriage. She is hindering her husband, her marriage, and her divine purpose.

By the way: The Women's Liberation Movement was not a God Movement.

Women's Empowerment Movement:

Today, there are many conferences in the corporate and Christian arena that are specifically designed for women. There are a significant number of books written for women by women, addressing areas such as: how to succeed in the corporate world, how to handle your own finances, and how to get want you want while climbing the corporate ladder of success. (I call it empowering women.) If you look on television today, what used to be male dominant professions, such as news and sports commentating, are now roles that are occupied by women. (I read that women make up fifty-one per cent in the business arena). Yes, you can definitely say that women are making a significant impact in today's world.

As a Christian, if you are attending any kind of conference or meeting that addresses women's empowerment, make sure that it doesn't run contrary to the Word of God or His divine order. Anyone speaking on empowerment had better come from the Word of God, edifying women, but also edifying the order of God. It is the will of the Lord for His daughters to better themselves, but it is not

His will for us to go against His order in our pursuit. If someone is telling you subtlety that you can do this and you don't need a man, listen to me very carefully and check the Holy Spirit within you, because He is going to guide you to the truth, which will make you free. If you are married, you must not do anything against your husband's wishes when it comes to major life decisions. This is why you better know for sure that you are ready to get married.

Women are very powerful beings. God created us to be this way. However, in that power, He also created order. Anything outside of the order He created is not of Him, but of the flesh. Like I said, whether you what to believe it or not, God's Word doesn't change, regardless of how we try to change it to suit our own personal agendas.

I know this may not go well; however, I have to say it. It is a mandate on me because many of us are out order and we are looking to others for direction, instead of looking to Jesus Christ and the Word of God. Listen with your spiritual heart and ears carefully, because in the natural this is a hard thing to swallow. If your assignment does not edify the Lord, His people, His Kingdom, or His order, there is a great possibility that you are not hearing from God. You might be walking in the flesh.

In the order of God my husband is my head, so I must listen to him when he wants me to stop doing something. Whether I agree with him or not, regardless, even if I know he is wrong, I must submit. My assignment cannot go against the order of God. *"Obedience is better than sacrifice," I Samuel 15:22 (NLT).* Pete and I operate as a team. We listen to each other, debate if necessary, work together, and come to conclusions together. Still this does not negate the order of God in the marriage. In the end, my husband has the final word. If I know for a fact that I've heard from the Lord and Pete is wrong, I immediately go into spiritual warfare, while submitting to his wishes. I know this is not easy to comprehend, but please listen with spiritual ears.

If your God-given assignment causes disruption in your house, ask this question "Is this of me or the Lord?" Your assignment or purpose in the Lord coincides with who your husband is. My assignment from the Lord must edify the Lord and enhance my husband. I am his help meet, he is not mine. If you believe that you are being called to do something that doesn't include your husband, I strongly believe you may have missed God. No matter how spiritual or anointed you think you are. It's just that simple. I am married to Pete; therefore, I don't have an assignment outside of Pete's vision. (By the way, I am referring to ministry; however, be careful in your job situation too. It should not take you away from your first responsibilities.)

If you know what the Lord is calling you to do and your husband can't see it, submit and wait on the Lord. If your husband is in error, it is God's responsibility to correct him, not yours. Your responsibility is to wait patiently for God, while praying for your husband. Two things will result from this, either you missed God, or His timing, or your husband will begin to see through the eyes of God what you said is correct and it is from the Lord. In both situations, everyone benefits, and no one is out of order.

I recalled years ago when I first informed Pete I was called to write, and work with women. At the time he couldn't see this. I had two choices, wait on God to reveal it to him, or go against the order of God, and do my own thing. There were people, from all perspectives, worldly and spiritual persuading me to just go ahead and not worry about Pete or his feelings. I didn't listen to their voices or the voice in my head. I submitted to the order of God. I knew I couldn't go against God's order, or I wasn't fitting into my husband's plan or the vision of the house. Was it easy to come to this conclusion? No. It was hard. But I know if I had gone along with my plans, not only would I have been out of order, but I would have missed the timing of God, shipwrecking myself and others who followed me. It's that serious! Now, years later both my husband and I see what God is doing in my life and our marriage, and now Pete is my biggest supporter. He is now telling me to go forth.

In summary, I do realize that these three areas are tough to accept. (In the beginning they were for me too. Why do you think it took ten years for me to say yes to the Lord?). They may be hard, but deep down, we know there is validity to this. As women of God it is time to get back to the things of God and His order. The world's way has hurt us for far too long. It has hindered our marriages, caused disruption in our families, misplaced our children, and more importantly tainted our walks with Jesus.

Choose you this day whom you will serve.... But as for me and my house, we will serve the Lord, Joshua 24:15 (KJV).

Chapter 5

Foolish Wives In The Bible Who Hindered Their Husbands

The Bible gives examples of women who were foolish and hindered their husbands. We've already talked about Eve, so here are a few more:

Rebekah: *(See Genesis 27: 2-14)*: (She is also mentioned in Romans 9:10)
Key Verses:
[2] "I am an old man now," Isaac said, "and I expect every day to be my last. [3] Take your bow and a quiver full of arrows out into the open country, and hunt some wild game for me. [4] Prepare it just the way I like it so it's savory and good, and bring it here for me to eat. Then I will pronounce the blessing that belongs to you, my firstborn son, before I die."[5] But Rebekah overheard the conversation. So when Esau left to hunt for the wild game, [6] she said to her son Jacob, "I overheard your father asking Esau [7] to prepare him a delicious meal of wild game. He wants to bless Esau in the Lord's presence before he dies. [8] Now, my son, do exactly as I tell you. [9] Go out to the flocks and bring me two fine young goats. I'll prepare your father's favorite dish from them. [10] Take the food to your father; then he can eat it and bless you instead of Esau before he dies."[11] "But Mother!" Jacob replied. "He won't be fooled that easily. Think how hairy Esau is and how smooth my skin is! [12] What if my father touches me? He'll see that I'm trying to trick him, and then he'll curse me instead of blessing me."[13] "Let the curse fall on me, dear son," said Rebekah. "Just do what I tell you. Go out and get the goats."[14] So Jacob followed his mother's instructions, bringing her the two goats. She took them and cooked a delicious meat dish, just the way Isaac liked it.

Rebekah started out with good intentions, but eventually she caused the demise of her relationship with her husband and two sons, causing strife between them. Her plot to assist God in making sure that her youngest and favored child received the first fruit blessing led her into deception. Believing what she was doing was right; she justified her actions in her attempt to bring what God said to pass. But no matter how much good she thought she was doing, she was wrong. Yes, Rebekah and Jacob got their own way, but they gained nothing that God would not have given them anyway. In the end, they both lost. She never saw her son, Jacob, again; and even though the Word doesn't get very specific, her relationship with her husband was probably never the same. Deception and mistrust came into the marriage, leaving in their wake irreparable damage. Blessings are given by God, not gained by deceit.

Potiphar's Wife: *(See Genesis 39: 6-20)*: **(NLT).**

[6]… Now Joseph was a very handsome and well-built young man. [7] And about this time, Potiphar's wife began to desire him and invited him to sleep with her. [8] But Joseph refused. "Look," he told her, "my master trusts me with everything in his entire household. [9] No one here has more authority than I do! He has held back nothing from me except you, because you are his wife. How could I ever do such a wicked thing? It would be a great sin against God." [10] She kept putting pressure on him day after day, but he refused to sleep with her, and he kept out of her way as much as possible. [11] One day, however, no one else was around when he was doing his work inside the house. [12] She came and grabbed him by his shirt, demanding, "Sleep with me!" Joseph tore himself away, but as he did, his shirt came off. She was left holding it as he ran from the house. [13] When she saw that she had his shirt and that he had fled, [14] she began screaming. Soon all the men around the place came running. "My husband has brought this Hebrew slave here to insult us!" she sobbed. "He tried to rape me, but I screamed. [15] When he heard my loud cries, he ran and left his shirt behind with me."[16] She kept the shirt with her, and when her husband came home that night, [17] she told him her story. "That Hebrew slave you've had around here tried to make a fool of me,"

she said. [18] "I was saved only by my screams. He ran out, leaving his shirt behind!" [19] After hearing his wife's story, Potiphar was furious! [20] He took Joseph and threw him into the prison where the king's prisoners were held.

Although not called by a name, Potipher's wife was a foolish woman. Bored and idle, she used her sexual and social power for evil purposes. Her lies and deceit resulted in an innocent and good man going to jail; which in the end disrupted the overall operations of her husband's assignment and their household. A wife who is idle, unfulfilled or deceitful is not only a hindrance to her husband, but others as well. We normally find these types of women as busybodies, gossipers, or backbiters. While their husbands are off doing good, they are off somewhere causing havoc or doing evil.

Jezebel: *(See 1 Kings 16:31 – 2 Kings 9:37):*
(Her name is used as a synonym for great evil in Revelation 2:20)

No one else so completely sold himself to what was evil in the Lord's sight as did Ahab, for his wife, Jezebel, influenced him. 1 Kings 21:25 (NLT)

(Jezebel, being void of any spiritual sensitivity and conscience, **urged** him **on** in evil.)

"Jezebel had great power. She not only managed her husband, but she also had over 850 pagan priests under her control. She was committed to her gods and getting anything she wanted. She believed in Supreme rule and reign, and killed an innocent man, Naboh, for his land. She ranks as one of the most evil women in the Bible. She was determined to make Israel and her husband worship her Gods.[3]

Jezebel used her great influence to turn her already wicked husband further from God. Her sins brought death to both her husband and to her. What's sad about the life of Jezebel is that here is a woman gifted and with great influence, but instead of using these traits for good by assisting and helping her husband, she used her gifts for evil. It was obvious that Jezebel was out of divine order because she portrayed the man in the marriage. I wonder how powerful her husband's kingdom could have been if she would have used her gifts and influence in a more positive manner? What if she would have helped her husband, instead of hindering him? Women are gifted for reasons. Our gifts are to enhance our husbands and the overall marriage.

Job's Wife: *(See Job 2:8-10): (NLT)*

Then Job scraped his skin with a piece of broken pottery as he sat among the ashes. [9] His wife said to him, "Are you still trying to maintain your integrity? Curse God and die."[10] But Job replied, "You talk like a godless woman. Should we accept only good things from the hand of God and never anything bad?" So in all this, Job said nothing wrong.

Job's wife's lack of spiritual insight and sympathy for her husband brought further hurt to his suffering. What he needed was her support, but what he received was her ridicule of his integrity and faith in God. When he was at his lowest point, instead of his wife encouraging him and being there for him, or even praying for him, she turned against him. How many of us are like Job's wife? A powerful woman once said, "It's easy to love a man when he has everything going for him, but when he is down and out, that's when he needs your love the most."

Herodias, Herod Antipas' Wife: *(See Matthew 14:1-11):*

[1] At that time Herod the tetrarch heard of the fame of Jesus, [2] And said unto his servants, This is John the Baptist; he is risen from the dead; and therefore mighty works do shew forth themselves in him. [3] For Herod had laid hold on John, and bound him, and put him in prison for Herodias' sake, his brother Philip's wife*. [4] For John said unto him, It is not lawful for thee to have her. [5] And when he would have put him to death, he feared the multitude, because they counted him as a prophet. [6] But when Herod's birthday was kept, the daughter of Herodias

danced before them, and pleased Herod. [7] Whereupon he promised with an oath to give her whatsoever she would ask. [8] And she, being before instructed of her mother, said, Give me here John Baptist's head in a charger. [9] And the king was sorry: nevertheless for the oath's sake, and them which sat with him at meat, he commanded it to be given her. [10] And he sent, and beheaded John in the prison. [11] And his head was brought in a charger, and given to the damsel: and she brought it to her mother.

Not only was this woman a hindrance to her current husband, she caused shame to her former husband, who by law she was still married too (*she left him for his brother). When confronted by John the Baptist of her adultery, instead of repenting, she became infuriated; and, sinned not only against John the Baptist, but also against God. Given the opportunity, she used her daughter to trick her husband into beheading John the Baptist. Although her husband didn't want to do it, she situated him in a position where he had no other option. She was a hindrance to her husband and his entire Kingdom.

Through deceit, lies, rebellion, ridiculing, blatant disobedience and disrespect, all of these women mentioned above played a vital (if not, specific) role in either destroying their husbands, or hindering them. Some never reached their full potential, fulfilling their assignments. And although some husbands were able to recover, the damage to the marriage was irreparable. Many times, as wives, we think that we have our husband's backs, or that we know best; however, often times, we never see the end results of our hindering spirits until it's too late.

Chapter 6
The Calling Of A Wife (Help Meet)

I told my husband that one of the hardest professions is that of a wife. Well, that is a God-fearing Christian wife. Why? A wife who is submitted to the Lord, His Word, and her husband is considered a fool by today's women. She is looked upon as deceived by the "foolishness" and suppression of religion and, instead of being envied; she is ridiculed by her peers.

I've already told you that when I was getting out the military, many of my Christian female friends thought that I was out of my mind for getting out of "my security blanket" to follow my husband. They couldn't believe the Lord had called me to do this. Some even questioned my decision and tried to persuade me not to do it. What they saw was an up and coming, successful military officer who had the potential to go far in the military, but was about to give it all up for a man- her husband. Even though they had read the scripture instructing wives to fit into their husbands' plans, or submit oneself to your husband, it was not easy for them to comprehend when one of their own actually did this.

As a Christian wife in today's world, we have so much competing against and distracting us. Just like the world, we want the designer clothes, the beautiful home, the newest technology, the fancy car, and the successful career with the pay to match. Instead of reading our Bibles and praying for our families, we are spending time on the Internet, Facebook, Twitter, texting, looking at television, working late hours at the office, or shopping at the mall. In regard to our spiritual development and growth, we have replaced or substituted prominent women of faith for advice and guidance, with new role models of women who don't portray or profess Jesus (not openly anyway). All of these are devices of satan; and, if we don't remain balanced or careful, they will keep us from reaching our God-ordained destiny.

For the most part, many of us want a man, and want to be married, but we don't want to be a wife. If truth be told, we want to be like Eve. That is why the man that finds a good wife is blessed. *"The man who finds a wife finds a treasure and receives favor from the Lord," Proverbs 18:22 (NLT)*. I guess I like this translation better because it explicitly tells me how a good wife is both a treasure and a blessing to her husband; and, more significantly, how the Lord is pleased with her, bestowing favor on the man for just having found her.

When the man is looking for a wife, he is looking for someone to assist and be with him, as he fulfills his God ordained assignment. He is searching for someone who is not only compatible with him, but also with his vision. That is why when the husband finds his wife, he knows he that has found a good thing. Out of all of the women he could have chosen, he chose his wife because he expected her to be a replica of what the Bible says a wife should be.

For this reason, I believe a wife is a calling, or a mission from God. And unfortunately, not every married woman has answered the call. And they can't without the help of the Holy Spirit. It was not easy for me to get out of the military. Even today, it is still hard for me to submit to my husband and do what the Lord commands me to do pertaining to him. To be honest, the only way I am able to do this, is by the power of the Holy Spirit. This is mainly because I yield myself under His authority. It takes God for me to be the help meet I am to be to my husband, abandoning my individuality, and yes to be honest, my selfish wants, desires and goals, in order for me to help my husband become the man God has ordained him to be. There are times when I want to go back to the things I want and desire, such as: my career and my way of doing things; especially, when I feel my husband doesn't appreciate me or is tak ing me for granted. However, because I am a godly wife, I answer to the call of God. It is not about my will, but His will be done.

I informed my husband how hard it was for me to write this book because people are going to think I have lost my mind. Women will anyway. I hardly believe the men will. In fact, they'll probably rejoice saying, "Finally, someone sees the light."

How can you tell a woman who is successful, making more money than the average person, and who is the essence of today's successful woman, to submit to her husband and help him? Just writing it sounds mind-boggling. She is not going to adhere to these words, because not only does she have it going on, but she is also a woman of power, and with a destination, and that destination does not include her husband. How can you tell her that success is not based on what she has accomplished from a worldly perspective, but how she obeyed God, submitted to her husband, while helping him to be successful? How can you tell her that yes her way seems better, but God's way is best? How can you tell her all of this, when everything she sees or hears is contrary to what thus said the Lord? It's not easy, but the truth of the matter, is that we as women were created to help man, not the other way around.

Marriage is divinely instituted by God, designed for the happiness of man (male and female), and established to replenish the earth's population. Therefore, when the man finds a wife, he marries her, and the two individuals become one in the marriage. Not losing their identities, they work together to fulfill the assignment (vision) for the house. The man needs his wife to assist him, cover him in prayer, and submit to him as he submits to God. He also needs her strengths to cover his weaknesses. The wife needs the husband to provide for her, keep her secure, and to love her as the weaker vessel. Her weaknesses are covered by his strengths; however, her strengths help her husband to be successful—thus, the two shall be one. Anything outside of this, will more than likely cause the wife to become a hin drance to her husband; regardless if she or her husband is aware of it.

Whether we want to believe it or not, when we stand at the altar professing our love for each other, we are answering a call into marriage: The calling of a husband and the calling of a wife. It takes the yielding of our flesh, submission to God and His Word and the help of the Holy Spirit to answer the call; otherwise, the possibility of a hindrance is great.

While I was bringing this book to a close and getting ready to send it to the publisher, something happened in our marriage that solidified my calling as a wife—a help meet. In the natural, you couldn't tell that anything had taken place, but in the spiritual realm there was a change. On this particular day, before my husband came home, I knew that I needed to speak with him about something important pertaining to me and where God was leading me. So, I prayed to the Lord for the Holy Spirit to guide my conversation, and to convey what I needed to say in a "nice manner"- sweet words soothing to his ears.

After dinner, we continued to sit at the table, and it was there when the Holy Spirit enabled me to share my heart to my husband. And as a result, my husband was able to share his heart to me. For the first time that I could remember, my husband heard my heart (not words, but my heart). And for the first time, it was there at that table, I saw my husband. Not a man, not Pete, but my husband. It was then that I knew I had crossed over, answered the call, and became his wife. I could now let everything go that I was trying to hold on to, and allow my husband to lead us into our God-ordained destiny. No, my husband didn't see the change, but I did. It was then at that moment that I knew I was no longer a hindrance. My initial tears of frustration, disobedience and resentment, turned into tears of peace, joy and obedience, emerging a woman who could finally say she is a help meet to her husband. Now I could release this book.

A wife is a calling from God, and it is time we answer the call and become the help meet we were ordained to be.

Conclusion

As guided by the Holy Spirit and God's Word I have attempted to convey to you what it means to be a help meet rather than a hindrance to your husband.

My mother always told me, "Do as I say, not as I did." I leave this message with you. Don't be like me. I wasted ten years of my marriage (my life period) in rebellion. I was trying to keep my ego intact, while unknowingly hindering my husband. Learn from me, and be the woman and the **Help Meet** for your husband that the Lord created you to be.

By the way, you are not alone. As women of God, we are in this together. We want you to succeed. It is imperative that you succeed. People are watching you: other saints, your family, your friends, and the world. And don't forget you have God's Holy Spirit to help you! He will enable you to be what God created you to be. Pray and ask Him how to be a help meet to your husband. Ask Him how to pray and what to pray for your husband. Ask Him to show you your husband, so that you can prepare for him daily. Ask Him how to submit to your husband and how to die to your goals, your dreams (for a season); in order for your husband to fulfill his God-given purpose, the vision God has assigned Him. Don't forget to inquire about your purpose and how it fits into your husband's plans. Ask Him today. He is just a prayer away. He is waiting on you.

Be blessed and know that I love you, and more importantly the Lord loves you.

If you are not saved, it is not a coincidence that you are reading this book. I petition you to ask the Lord to come into your heart right now. All you have to do is repent of your sins and turn your back on the world. You must believe in your heart and confess with your mouth that Jesus Christ is Lord, and that He died and rose for you so you can have everlasting life with Him (Romans 10: 9-10). If you have done so, and now feel warmth surging all over your body, Dear Heart you are Born Again. Welcome to the Body of Christ, the Kingdom of God and a personal relationship with Jesus.

Notes

Part Two: Submission: What God Word Says About Submission ...?

1. Neil T. Anderson & Charles Mylander, The Christ-Centered Marriage, Regal Books (Division of Gospel Light), © 1996, Chapter 1: God's Perfect Design*

2. Spirit Filled Bible, KJV, 1991/1995 ©, pgs. 1846-1847 (Under Kingdom Dynamics, Section 3:1)

Part Four: Foolish Wives in the Bible Who Hindered Their Husbands

3. Life Application Study Bible, NLT, 1996, Tyndale, Segments from the Bible (Commentary on Jezebel, Page 551)

*Bible study notes and quotes from WordSeach Program Version 5/7, NavPress,

About the Author

Born and raised in Baltimore, Maryland, Fannie A. Pierce always knew she had a purpose in life, but didn't know what it was. After graduating from high school in 1982, not knowing what to do, she joined the Army Reserves. It was there the term "Be All You Can Be" became real to her. After the reserves, she attended Bowie State University, Bowie, Maryland. At Bowie, she joined the school's Reserves Officer Corps' Training (R.O.T.C.) Program. After graduation she was commissioned as an officer in the United States Army.

After a combined total of 14 years in the military, both active/non active, the Lord called her out of the armed forces. Diligently seeking the Lord, it was there, in the summer of 2005, the Lord clearly told her to start a publishing company. Although her passion and tranquility was always writing, she never in her wildest dreams considered starting a publishing company. After 4 long years, due to fear and not knowing anything about the publishing business, she finally submitted to God. It is when she gave it all up; she finally found her passion and purpose.

Fannie is called to three things: To be a God-fearing woman, to be a wife to her husband and to minister to God's Daughters.

Fannie lives in Dothan, Alabama with her husband, Pete Pierce Jr., of twenty wonderful years and their German Shepherd Max. Both are both Ordained Elders at Northview Christian Church, Dothan, Alabama.

www.ingramcontent.com/pod-product-compliance
Lightning Source LLC
Chambersburg PA
CBHW050558300426
44112CB00013B/1973